The Freedom Movement:

Free Food, Free Drugs & World Peace

The Freedom Movement:

Free Food, Free Drugs & World Peace

Ethan James

iUniverse, Inc.
Bloomington

The Freedom Movement: Free Food, Free Drugs & World Peace

iUniverse books may be ordered through booksellers or by contacting:

iUniverse
1663 Liberty Drive
Bloomington, IN 47403
www.iuniverse.com
1-800-Authors (1-800-288-4677)

ISBN: 978-1-4620-2593-0 (pbk)
ISBN: 978-1-4620-2594-7 (ebk)

Printed in the United States of America

iUniverse rev. date: 06/30/2011

Contents

FOREWORD

This book is intended for entertainment purposes only. The author does not assume any responsibility for misinterpretation or misuse of ideas presented in this book. This book is not intended for sale to minors. Reader discernment is encouraged.

Dedicated to the People of the Free World

'Buying is a profound pleasure.' ~ *Simone de Beauvoir*

'A free market system allows all parties to compete, which ensures the best and most competitive project emerges, and ensures a fair, democratic process.' ~ *Sarah Palin*

'Expose yourself to your deepest fear; after that, fear has no power, and the fear of freedom shrinks and vanishes. You are free.' ~ *Jim Morrison*

'I am convinced that the path to a new, better and possible world is not capitalism, the path is socialism.'
~ *Hugo Chávez*

'When fools hear of the Way, they laugh out loud at it. If they didn't laugh, it couldn't be called the Way.'
~ *Lao-Tzu*

'All drugs of any interest to any moderately intelligent person in America are now illegal.' ~ *Thomas Szasz*

'A people free to choose will always choose peace.'
~ *Ronald Reagan*

'A dream you dream alone is only a dream. A dream you dream together is reality.' ~ *John Lennon*

Preface

Do you want to be able to eat as much food as you want without paying? Wouldn't you like to download all the videos and music in the world for free? Wouldn't you like tickets to go to movies, music shows, and sporting events for free? What I am presenting is a new socioeconomic theory built upon a simple premise: People should be able to "buy" these things for free and companies should still be able to make real money. This sounds like a crime doesn't it? Not to worry, the underlying structure of the money-based economy can still remain intact, and indeed, some things you will still need to pay for with real money, such as illegal drugs.

The very first line of The Communist Manifesto states: "The history of all hitherto existing society is the history of class struggles." Nowhere are these class struggles more sharply contrasted than in the struggle for resources, which are based on scarcity. The greatest absurdity is starvation and malnourishment despite worldwide industrialization.

The time has come for food competition in the world market to be reduced, and the only way that this can be accomplished is if food is "sold" for free. Previously, food aid has been considered a loss, but my socioeconomic theory allows for real profit to be generated. What this means is that food aid can be "bought" for free everywhere in the world without significant losses in revenue. Individual governments will be allowed to regulate as per usual. In this way, the world food and stock markets will remain intact, food "prices" will still be calculated according to inflation, and real profits will still be generated.

As a result of food socialization, most other commodities would be made free as well in the corporate sphere. Independently run businesses, however, would not be completely socialized. Thus, my socioeconomic theory provides a new model that allows socialism and capitalism to function together harmoniously.

I present the socioeconomic theory in the first chapter. The following chapters provide an examination of the state of the world's politics and economy. Many countries are struggling with development—these are the nations on which I've decided to focus. In some cases, I have presented political solutions and in others economic solutions.

All you have to do is read on and accept if you want to become a part of the peaceful worldwide socioeconomic revolution.

CHAPTER 1

The Socioeconomic Theory

In a nutshell, my socioeconomic theory argues for the socialization of cheap and necessary commodities, however, small businesses will be protected and most forms of labor and pay will remain unaffected. Real property will, for the most part, cost real money and therefore will not be free.

The Corporate Revolution

Because many corporations sell other cheap items alongside food in their business chains, for purposes of ease most of these consumable items and cheap commodities should be made free as well. Cheap items sold by corporations that should be socialized and made free include, but may not be limited to: bottled water, fast-food, grocery items such as beer, cigarettes, condoms, paperback books, magazines, comics, greeting cards, cheap drugs, cheap clothes, and cheap electronics. A problem arises though. Once there is an elimination of cost to the consumer, demand will be completely uninhibited.

Free & Socialized Grocery Items in Developed Countries

This theory would be useless if there was no way to limit demand to a reasonable level. The solution is quite simple: a mass survey must be conducted in every city, state and country in order to determine free food budgets per household size. Worldwide Internet accounts will contain customer information and item credits issued by national governments and federal reserves for free food. Additionally, identity scan cards must be implemented in order to curtail demand to a reasonable level. In this way, corporations can continue their global expansion as per the status quo and consumers can continue to "purchase" goods as they normally do, with one important catch—they will be free. In this way, demand for food in corporate chains will be permanently limited to the current demand level as determined by surveys.

Worldwide Surveys

Worldwide surveys must be conducted to determine how much food per household is consumed per increment of time (probably a month) in each nation. The size of the household must obviously also be determined in the survey. Changes in household size can be filed with your state government if you need to update your info in the worldwide database.

Internet Customer Accounts

Since all consumables in corporate chains will be free, they will be considered equal value. Therefore each consumable item will simply be treated as an item credit in your account. You might have, for instance, 800 item credits allotted to your account per month based on your household size. Item credits will be carried over into the next month if they are unused. In this way, you can save items credits indefinitely.

Universal Scan Card

Universal identity cards will link you to your account at various corporate chains all across the world. Most likely, your driver's license will become your shopping card in your home country.

The Bottom Line For Companies

From a consumer perspective, all free consumable items are of equal value, however, from the perspective of the seller, they are *not* of equal value. As a result of this, risk is almost completely eliminated for businesses that sell free items. The extent of government regulations for free item credits, based upon household size, depends on individual nations' laws.

Items in Corporate Chains That Will Not Be Free

Since many corporate chains sell items that are real property made from scarce resources, these items must *not* be free. These items include, but may not be limited to:

1. Firearms.
2. Expensive Sound Systems and Home Entertainment Systems.
3. Computers, Laptops, Plasma TVs, Video Game Systems, Cellphones, etc.

4. Expensive Tools.
5. Expensive Musical Equipment.
6. Furniture and Kitchen Appliances.
7. Jewelry.
8. Expensive clothes.

These kinds of items will be separated and marked with prices. These items will still have barcodes and the circumstances of buying and selling will remain unchanged.

Other Consumables that Will Not be Free:

1. Electric Power.
2. Natural Gas.
3. Oil.
4. Water Utility.

Electric Power, Natural Gas, Oil and Water Utilities cannot be "sold" for free since they are scarce resources that are quickly being depleted.

The Internet Revolution

Music and videos will be free to download, and will generate real profit for the businesses and performers. There will be *unlimited* demand for these intangible products since they are 100% digital. Piracy laws must be strictly enforced.

Other Real Property That Will Not Be Free

1. Housing, Stores.

2. Planes, Tanks, Cars, SUVs, Boats, etc.
3. Rocket Launchers, Grenades, Guns and Other Projectile Weapons.

Housing cannot be "sold" for free because certain variables including labor, time, cost, and scarcity of available land space must be taken into consideration. Planes, Tanks, Cars, SUVs, and Boats cannot be "sold" for free since they depend on oil, a scarce resource that is quickly being depleted. Rocket Launchers, Grenades and Guns are dangerous and cannot be free.

Protection of Independent and Small Businesses

Some independently owned and operated businesses will remain unaffected and their merchandise will NOT be free since they are made from scarce resources. For instance, independently run jewelry stores, expensive clothes stores, and expensive restaurants will remain entirely unaffected and will still require real money and/or credit cards. Mom and pop stores will be partly socialized, depending on the merchandise. For instance, independently run gas stations will charge money for gas but candy bars and other snacks will be free. To paraphrase Marx: Entrepreneurs of the world unite!

The Affects of the Revolution on Services

Preservation of the World Stock Markets, Banking, and Mortgage Lending

All world stock markets will remain structurally intact. All behaviors of buying, selling and trading in the stock markets will remain entirely unaffected. All world, government, and private banking will remain completely unaffected. Mortgage lending and all other forms of money lending will remain completely unaffected by the revolution.

Most Service Jobs Will Remain Unaffected

Most service jobs will simply remain unaffected by the socioeconomic revolution. Real Estate Lending will remain entirely unaffected. Labor rights and freedom will continue as per the status quo. For instance, paid laborers such as carpenters, plumbers and electricians will conduct business as usual. Private practice lawyers, surgeons, and specialty doctors such as proctologists will remain entirely unaffected by the socioeconomic revolution. Federal, state, and city jobs will remain unaffected.

Other Services

Some services will remain unaffected, and others might be socialized.

1. Low cost healthcare may be free, but high cost healthcare will not be free due to lack of qualified physicians.

2. Education may or may not be free. This depends entirely on local, state, and national governments.
3. Cheap tickets for sporting events, movie theatres, music venues and museums should probably be free everywhere in the world. Demand for tickets would increase since the "buyer" does not need to use real money, thus improving sales for performers and businesses alike.
4. Telecommunications and all other public utilities will remain unaffected and will not be free because they depend on scarce resources.
5. Satellite and cable will remain unaffected and will *not* be free.

A Message to The United States of America

Marijuana and hashish should be legalized and legally distributed as a free commodity. Hashish shops could be opened up in the United States, thus offering a new opportunity for business entrepreneurs. This is the only radical reform that I am calling for in the United States of America.

Conclusion

In many ways, technology plays a huge part in this revolution. Before the advent of computers, this idea would not have been possible, but the digital revolution has significantly changed the way that money is transferred and transacted. The basis for this revolution is simply this: The Internet is an intangible "virtual reality" that has made worldwide accounts and transfer of funds almost instantaneous. Internet Databases will be crucial to accessing accounts for free food and other free consumables.

Will cash based economy eventually be replaced? The answer to this question is unequivocally no. I'm not advocating for a completely credit based economy, and indeed, this is impossible, as many countries, such as Ukraine, are still primarily cash based.

On this note, the behavior of the world markets will, for the most part, remain entirely unaffected by the socioeconomic revolution. Labor and economic freedom will be upheld, all the same items and conveniences you are used to will be purchased as usual, with one crucial difference—lots of stuff will be free and thus easier to obtain. Don't forget—free booze and free digital downloads just might be the best part of this socioeconomic theory!

CHAPTER 2

Asia

In all of Asia, Japan, the world's 3rd largest economy, sets the example for both human development and freedom from corruption. The recent tsunami that hit the country could cost as much as $300 billion in repairs, and radiation contamination will be an ongoing concern. While this is a tremendous setback, Japan is destined to make an economic comeback with the help of foreign aid.

After Nixon opened up China in the 70's, the country pursued a more open-market economy, which it has continued to successfully develop, and, although it is the number one "world leader in gross value of industrial output"[1], China is still working towards achieving high human development.

India is currently "developing into an open-market economy" and struggling to improve human development for its population of 1.2 billion.[2]

South Korea has, since the 1960s, "achieved an incredible record of growth and global integration to become a high-tech industrialized economy."[3]

Southeast Asian nations are home to a very diverse population of ethnic groups and indigenous peoples; the economies of its various nations are just as diverse. One thing they all have in common is corruption.

Bangladesh

Bangladesh, one of the most populous countries on the planet, suffers from extreme corruption, although there have been some improvements in recent years. From the 2011 Index of Economic Freedom: "Corruption remains a serious impediment to investment and economic growth. By some estimates, off-the-record payments by firms result in an annual loss of 2-3 percent of GDP. Given that corruption blights all other economic freedoms, this continues to be a key area for improvement."[4]

Bangladesh's environmental issues, such as devastating floods and cyclones, along with corrupt practices in administration of land, have driven millions of Bangladeshis into homelessness. About 4.5 million are "completely landless" at this time,[5] which contributes to poverty and "expansion of slums with all affiliated social problems."[6] Although Bangladeshi law stipulates that government-owned land is to be distributed to the poor and landless, influential people fraudulently grab rural land, according to a spokesperson for the Association for Land Reforms and Development.[7] From Bangladesh's Land Law: "Where in the rural area any khas land fit for being used as homestead is available, the Government shall, in settling such land, give preference to landless farmers and labourers."[8] Fraud, bribery, and favoritism play a large part in land grabbing.[9]

Access to clean water and food is a crisis in Bangladesh. Currently, 65 million Bangladeshis don't have enough food, and although the country has made improvements in cessation of hunger[10], the situation could easily turn into tragic starvation, as is the case in India. Considering that Bangladesh is rated by Transparency International as more corrupt than India, its probably safe to say that government corruption and negligence are taking food away from the hungry and impoverished. Should the government decide to further address the issue, adopting solutions similar to those that I've discussed for India could solve the problem of water pollution in Bangladesh.

In addition to improving enforcement of landlaws and food distribution, the government should also focus on raising literacy rates, which are astonishingly low for a country that is swiftly approaching average human development status. It is unlikely that any of these reforms will happen, however, until the government first deals with internal corruption. Despite significant corruption, my socioeconomic theory will still work in Bangladesh.

Burma

Although Burma is a multi-party state, it is primarily controlled by a military regime operating under the Union Solidarity and Development Party. Burmese law is based on the British legal system, but the country has gone through several constitutions since 1988. Corruption continues to undermine Burma's development:

> Burma, a resource-rich country, suffers from pervasive government controls, inefficient economic policies, corruption, and rural poverty. Burma's poor investment climate hampers the inflow of foreign investment; in recent years, foreign investors have shied away from nearly every sector except for natural gas, power generation, timber, and mining. The exploitation of natural

resources does not benefit the population at large.[11]

For the sake of consolidation of power, the oppressive regime of the USDP has caused a humanitarian crisis in Burma:

> The Burmese military continues to direct attacks on civilians in ethnic areas, particularly in Karen, Karenni, and Shan states of eastern Burma, and parts of western Burma in Chin and Arakan states. Abuses by the Burmese military against civilians in violation of international humanitarian law include the widespread use of anti-personnel landmines, sexual violence against women and girls, extrajudicial killings, forced labor, torture, beatings, targeting of food production and means of civilian livelihood, and confiscation of land and property.[12]

It is highly unlikely that my ideas will be appealing to the Burmese government.

International pressure will be required to reform Burma's government and transform its economy.

Cambodia

Cambodia suffers from extensive corruption at the hands of the Cambodian People's Party (CPP), a result of the legacy left behind by over a decade of Vietnamese occupation. A lack of human and property rights characterize Cambodia;

its government neglects nearly a third of the country's population who currently live below the poverty line.

Cambodia's Indochine Mining Ltd is located primarily in Ratanakiri Province, one of the least developed of all its provinces, where rural poverty and disease cause nearly 1 in 4 children die before the age of five.[13] In this regard, the mining situation in Cambodia is not much different than in India or most of Africa—poor subsistence farming communities are displaced or neglected while the state plunders valuable minerals out from under them.

The greatest opposition to the CPP is the Sam Rainsy Party, whose members espouse personalist philosophy. This movement is small at the moment but will become incredibly important in counterbalancing collectivist political ideology in Cambodia.

China

China is a quickly developing nation—an economic giant poised to dominate the global market. In 2010, China was rated the 2nd largest economy; the dollar value of its agricultural and industrial output finally eclipsed that of The United States of America.[14] Despite China's success in developing a market-base economy, extreme poverty remains endemic:

> 21.5 million rural population live below the official "absolute poverty" line (approximately \$90 per year); an additional 35.5 million rural population live above that level but below the official "low income" line (approximately \$125 per year).[15]

Much of China's success in the global market is the result of the political-economic policies that came with its independence in 1949, and the Democratic Republic of China's social revolution—The Great Leap Forward, also known as "The Big Rush". The PRC's policies focused on socialist heavy industry, whereby resources became restricted by state control, and the government enforced rapid rural industrialization; opposition to the government was punishable by death.

Although historians still debate the exact number of peasants who died during the Great Leap Forward, estimates place the number who died by starvation at 35-45 million, and violent deaths (including torture, murder, and suicide) at approximately 3-5 million. Most people are astonished to learn of the cruelty of far-left authoritarianism in the PRC's history; what they may not know is that re-education and prison-labor camps centers still exist to this day in China. World leaders and organizations such as the UN's International Labor Organization call China's human rights policies into question.

Re-Education Centers

China's ongoing human rights violations stem in part from the Communist Party's ideology, such as the motto 'Collectivism before Individual', and 'Reform through Labor'. These mottos continue to play a part in communist China's political identity; movements based upon individualism are not tolerated.

One of the most persecuted groups are the adherents of the Falun Gong spiritual movement, which is based upon slow breathing, meditation, and has a moral philosophy grounded in truthfulness. Falun Gong started in the early

1990's and quickly became popular in Jilin province. Problems with China's government started around 1996, when practitioners of Falun Gong began writing literature that was deemed subversive in nature. In 1999, when the number of practitioners of the Falun Gong reached about 70 million—many of them began protesting for the right to practice their religion.[16] In response, China banned the religion and began arbitrarily incarcerating millions of Falun Gong in re-education and other detention centers.[17] More recent estimates place the number of Falun Gong in labor camps at hundreds of thousands.[18]

In the re-education centers, Falun Gong were subjected to psychiatric abuse, wherein they were brainwashed with government propaganda. Former convicts allege that practitioners were also subjected to a variety of tortures, including electroshock therapy, force-feeding, branding, and stress positions.[19] The Coalition to Investigate the Persecution of Falun Gong, an NGO led by former Canadian Secretary of State for the Asia-Pacific region David Kilgour and attorney David Matas, dug up evidence in 2006 that unethical organ harvesting was being conducted on innocent Falun Gong. According to the Kilgour-Matas report, doctors at prison camps were harvesting organs from live Falun Gong detainees, after matching transplant recipients in their databases.[20] Chinese doctors in Laogai prison camps also have illegally harvested organs from executed prisoners.[21] Organs that were harvested after execution included hearts, corneas, kidneys, and livers.[22]

'Laogai': Prison-labor Camps

Although China has closed many of its prison-labor camps, there are still two main regions where Laogai are still active: the Tibetan Autonomous Region and Qinghai—the two largest regions in China. Past research on the subject has shown that the living conditions in these prisons have been inhumane. Prisoners have been underfed, and assigned to overcrowded cells with cement, wood, or straw floors.[23] The most reprehensible aspect of Laogai camps is the imprisonment of political dissidents. According to the Laogai Research Foundation:

> Although many of the Laogai's prisoners are incarcerated for ordinary crimes, there is little respect for due process, or the rule of law in general, within the Chinese criminal justice system, meaning conviction by a fair trial is, at worst, impossible, and at best, uncertain in China. Many find themselves in the Laogai for crimes that are political in nature, such as 'subverting State power' or 'revealing state secrets'. The definitions of these crimes are so broad that the authorities can use them to justify arresting just about anyone for the most innocuous of activities, leading to a widespread suppression of all forms of expression.[24]

Since many of the Laogai prison camps are located in Tibet, it is no surprise that many of the people incarcerated in these prisons want freedom for their autonomous region. In March of 2009, the Laogai Museum in Washington D.C. ran a special exhibition revealing to the public "the use of the Laogai and prisons as a tool of repression within Tibet as well as other human rights abuses occurring within Tibet today, including arbitrary detention, torture and religious and political repression."[25] There are numerous examples of such detentions in the past few years. For example, Dhondup Wangchen, a Tibetan filmmaker, was arrested in 2008 for filming documentaries about Tibetans living under Chinese rule, and in 2009 was sentenced to a Laogai labor camp.[26] Another example is Netizen Dasher, another Tibetan who, after taking photographs and writing about the Tibetan Protests in 2008, was convicted of separatism and sentenced to 5 years at a prison camp in 2010.[27] Both of these men were tortured before being sentenced to imprisonment in the Chinese labor camps.

Prison Labor as a Means of Production

As difficult as it may be to face the issue openly and honestly, prison labor provides China with a very cheap source of production. Its usefulness as a means of production must be considered:

> The Laogai is more than a place to detain and 'reform' convicts and dissidents; it is inextricably linked to the Chinese economy. The Chinese government profits handsomely from the labor camp system by allowing goods made with forced labor to enter both domestic and international markets.[28]

Whereas China's economy depended entirely upon such forced labor during the Cultural Revolution, it accounts for a much smaller portion now. Clearly, China is on the path to eliminating prison labor altogether. Considering that the prison camps provide essential labor for China, it is inconceivable for the country to cease operations immediately. Instead, a phase-out reform should be initiated. In the meantime, there are several solutions to improving human rights in prison-labor camps:

1. Improve working conditions.
2. Improve judicial rulings by providing fair trials and upholding *habeus corpus*, in accordance with international law.
3. Release of political and religious dissidents.

Black Jails

Laogai prison camps are not the only places where dissidents are incarcerated; China also has a system called "black jails". According to a 2009 report, "the black jails are generally used to detain people who travel to Beijing and other cities to petition the government for redress of injustices faced in the countryside."[29] What's worse is that the detainees are tortured and beaten instead of having their grievances resolved. Reliable statistics on how many people are currently incarcerated in China's black jails are not readily available, in part because China is unwilling to admit to their existence.[30]

Censorship

Imprisonment is not the Communist Party's only solution to repressing dissidents; censorship has also been another useful method to enforce conformity and suppress religious or social thought that conflicts with government policy. China's censorship of media is the most far-reaching in all the nations of the world, and includes Internet, text messaging, instant messaging, television, film, video games, radio, literature, and all other forms of printed materials. Although Hong Kong is autonomous from mainland China, it has tried to curry favor with its mainland counterpart by practicing self-censorship:

> Certain media have been acquired by big businesses. They are no longer public instruments. They are now personal properties. They have very close economic ties with China, which funnels benefits to them. Some of them also have government backgrounds, even in sensitive departments such as the Ministry of National Security.[31]

Political-Economic Reform

Despite these grievous errors in China's political and judicial system, the Communist Party's latest plenary proposals promise to push the country's reform in a positive direction. The Five Year Guideline for 2011-2015 includes a section entitled: Protection of Labor Rights, in which the government promises to "enhance the enforcement of labor laws" and "improve working conditions".[32] In another section called Health Reforms, China's government also promises to "focus on improving community health-care services as its health-care reforms gather pace in the next five years".[33] Among financial reforms, the government promises to raise minimum wages, uphold public ownership, and encourage the growth of non-state owned enterprises.

Probably the best item on the table in China's Five Year Plan is improvement of rural infrastructure. The government proposed to "continue to improve rural public services and infrastructure construction, such as irrigation works and power grids, construct homes for needy people, improve the quality of rural compulsory education and health services, raise social security standards in rural regions and support poverty-stricken farmers."[34]

Charter 08

There is still more hope for the country. On December 10th, 2008, a radical new manifesto promising freedom for China was printed. Its original signatories included lawyers, bloggers, a former senior Communist Party official, and Liu Xiaobo, the charter's main author, who also won the 2010 Nobel Peace Prize. The Charter 08 calls for 19 specific demands:

1. Amending the Constitution.
2. Separation of Powers.
3. Legislative Democracy.
4. Independent Judiciary.
5. Public Control of Public Servants.
6. Guarantee of Human Rights.
7. Election of Public Officials.
8. Abolition of the Hukou System.
9. Freedom of Association.
10. Freedom of Assembly.
11. Freedom of Expression.
12. Freedom of Religion.
13. Civic Education.
14. Free Markets and Protection of Private Property.
15. Financial and Tax Reform.
16. Social Security Reform.
17. Protection of the Environment.

18. A Federated Republic.
19. Truth in Reconciliation.

The demands of Charter 08 clearly reveal that China is a nation struggling with freedom; its main author Liu Xiaobo is still currently imprisoned by China's government. If some of Charter 08's demands were fulfilled, China would be put on the path to becoming the next Russia. Obviously, the demands of Charter 08 are of such great importance that it should not go overlooked by the West.

Conclusion

The bottom line is this: The Chinese Communist Party needs a complete overhaul, starting with Charter's 08's 1st and 2nd demands, which call for the amendment of China's constitution and the separation of political parties. That being said, my socioeconomic platform will work in China no matter what the outcome.

India

India has long been subject to political conflict and environmental disasters—as a result of this the indigenous people of India have suffered greatly. Historically there have been periods of drought during summer monsoon seasons, which have led to millions of deaths as a result of famine. For example, the Bengal famine of 1770 led to deaths of 10 million peasants, the 1876-1877 famine claimed over 5 million lives, and the Bengal Famine of 1943 killed about 3 million peasants. You may notice that the numbers have dropped in the last few centuries. Technological and social revolution have both played a role in reducing deaths due to drought and famine, yet both still remain a crisis for millions of India's indigenous people, particularly the untouchables. Government negligence and corruption are obstacles to improving infrastructure and sustainability; thus malnourishment and disease persist in India. Currently, malnutrition affects 10-19% of India's population,[35] and 2 million children die from malnourishment every year.[36]

Background of the Ongoing Food Crisis

In the 1990's, a new, troubling trend took place; increased reports that farmers were committing suicide in Vidarbha, Maharasthra spread throughout the various states of India, and a crisis was declared. It was discovered that famine was the root cause of the suicides in Vidarbha. In response, the government of Maharasthra started providing *ex gratia* grants of approximately 100,000 ruples ($2000 US) for the families of suicide farmers. Unfortunately, this hasn't stopped farmers from committing suicide. The Prime Ministers of Maharasthra have drafted many relief packages with the approval of the World Trade Organization (WTO), however, international critics cite that there is ineffective representation of poor farmers in the drafting of these packages. In the meantime, 45,000 children die every year from malnutrition in Maharasthra[37], many of them belonging to suicide farmers.

Palagummi Sainath, an Indian journalist and expert on rural poverty, has said, "Beyond the sensationalism of news headlines and the reports of distress and starvation, is the tragedy of a population that has been consistently deprived of its rights and entitlements."[38] Furthermore, he argues that Maharasthra's state government Public Distribution System is corrupt; there are record numbers of grain (235 million tons) being harvested and stored by the government for export in the global market, yet much of the grain is rotting.[39] Sainath has pointed out that laws passed by the government of Maharasthra fail to adequately address the problem of starvation. For instance, Maharasthra state's Act entitled "The Maharasthra Deletion of the Term 'Famine' Act, 1963" asserts that "there is now no scope for famine conditions to develop".[40] Obviously this Act, which hasn't even been updated since 1963, hasn't done much to alleviate the suffering of the 45,000 starving children in the state.

Maharasthra is the wealthiest state in India; Mumbai currently is home to the world's tallest building, Burj Khalifa, which cost $1.5 billion to build. However, rural poverty is still severe in the smallest of its villages, such as Melghat, where grain distribution has officially ended; the people of Melghat must walk three miles to obtain grains, and an estimated 500 children die every year from starvation.[41] In the course of researching the crisis, I found a quote that sums up Maharasthra government corruption very succinctly: "Regions of Maharasthra reel under crop failures, debt, suicides, starvation, and high infant mortality, though the same state produces movies on colossal budgets and weddings of the rich last a fortnight."[42]

Internal Displacement

Another problem that contributes to poverty and famine is the displacement of Adivasis and other indigenous people. Adivasis are the hunter-gathers who, since Indian independence in 1947, have gradually had their forest rights taken away.[43] They can no longer eat from the forests, which have since become National Reserves, and continue to be displaced in order to make room for thousands of mining operations in India. In 2011, there were approximately 2000 mining leases and 550 prospecting leases being negotiated in Jharkhand state alone.[44] To date, 30 million people have been displaced by mining activities; 60% of them are scheduled tribes and OBC's.[45] The Ministry of Environment and Forests (MoEF) is overburdened with approximately 20,000 cases of illegal mining activities, many of which include deforestation of lands that the tribes have depended upon for generations.[46] As if this wasn't enough conflict, the indigenous people are also dragged into an ongoing war with Naxalite insurgents called Operation Green Hunt.

The Naxalites are Maoist extremists who champion the rights of the poor and scheduled tribes of India. They have attempted to thwart government sponsored mining projects in the forests of the "Red Corridor", which comprises many regions within the states of Maharasthra, Chhattisgarh, Orissa, and Andhra Pradesh. However, their extremist tactics have only drawn the ire of the various governments of India. In response to the terrorist acts in the Corridor, the government launched a paramilitary operation against the rebels called "Operation Green Hunt" in November of 2009. The conflict has only worsened recently: "In 2010, the Naxalites, operating in seven states, killed more than 100 police and paramilitary personnel in 2010, prompting a massive government security response."[47] Adivasis and other scheduled tribes are often caught in the crossfire between Naxal rebels and paramilitary strikes.

To make matters worse, there is another movement called the Salwa Judum, a group the wants to bring about an end to the Naxalite violence in their regions. The Salwa Judum is conducting war upon innocent tribespeople, whom they blame for the Naxalite movement, and continue to force them into displacement. The Salwa Judum torch their villages,[48] rape the women, and kill men among tribespeople such as the Adivasis, since they erroneously assume that they are compliant with the violent insurgency of the Naxalites. Clearly, the problem is complex, and the Salwa Judum is only bringing more horror and violence upon the Adivasis.

Water Scarcity

Another issue confronting Indian people is lack of clean water; there are tens of millions of people currently without clean water in the country. During my research on India, I stumbled upon a fascinating development in Singapore's wastewater treatment facilities. Sembcorp, in conjunction with Singapore's Public Utilities Board, began research on developing revolutionary facilities, which, through a four-stage process turn raw sewage into reclaimed water that is clean enough to drink. Research began in 1998 and the first two facilities opened in 2004 and 2007 under the brand name NEWater. Singapore's largest NEWater plant opened in July 2009, and only cost $180 million to build[49], which is only about $20-40 million more dollars than an average desalination plant. India can certainly find room in its budget to develop similar facilities, and should employ as many as possible in order to provide potable water.

Conclusion

Adivasis, Dalits, untouchables, scheduled tribes, and OBC's (Other Backward Classes) are all names for poor indigenous people of India. Historically, India's government has discriminated against all of them based upon class. More recently, the Indian government has taken positive strides to help OBC's, such as The Prevention of Atrocities

Act (POA), 1989, in which the Indian government outlawed crimes against scheduled tribes. The POA sounds like it has promise in preventing mass persecution of discriminated classes; in practice it has only helped to resolve minor disputes. Instead of pragmatically addressing class issues in a meaningful way, India's Supreme Court has upheld verdicts using ideas such as the "creamy layer" theory.

Tangible solutions are needed to improve living conditions for the impoverished in India. Fortunately, my socioeconomic theory partially solves the problem of famine in India since grain can be distributed through public distribution systems for free. Whereas Maharasthra used to hold on to grain in order to wait for the best offer, they can distribute it to the poor and needy in their state without significant loss.

India's famine problem can also be partially alleviated by connecting more villages to the main power grids. According to *The Times* (London), 400 million Indians do not have access to electricity[50], and about 56% of them live in rural areas[51] where many are willing to pay the high prices but still have not been connected. Increasing rural electrification will improve the lives of ordinary people throughout India.

Until pervasive corruption in the Indian government is weeded out, the poor will continue to suffer indefinitely. Above all, the ongoing crises in India point out that Indian state governments need to better administer to the poor classes. Ghandi would be appalled at the lack of progress India has thus far made in providing for the untouchables and other poor classes.

Indonesia

Indonesia, a majority Muslim country, suffers from poverty, corruption, and human rights violations. It is the fourth most populated country in the world. 13% of its population of 245 million people lives below the poverty line, and the per capita GDP is just $4,300.[52] Malnourishment is a continuing crisis in Indonesia, and currently affects 10-19% of the population.[53]

Corruption is on the rise in Indonesia: "far-reaching corruption in the national police has been exposed by a series of recent scandals involving bribery, intimidation, and the fabrication of evidence."[54] According to a senior researcher for Transparency International in Indonesia, "costly political campaigns and increasing party expenditures for legislative elections and local polls . . . have caused the general allocation funds for the education and public works sectors" to disappear into the pockets of "public officials in the executive and legislative bodies."[55] Indonesian President Susilo Bambang Yudhoyono "paid off judges not to press charges against political allies and hired intelligence forces to spy on his opponents."[56]

Property and Human Rights Violations

Property rights in Indonesia are not based on common law. For instance, there is "lack of clear land titles and the inability to own land in 'fee simple'.[57] Indonesia's judiciary is inefficient and corrupt: "Rulings can be arbitrary and inconsistent. Judges have been known to ignore contracts and rule against foreigners in commercial disputes. It is difficult to get the courts to enforce international arbitration awards. Enforcement of intellectual property rights is weak."[58] Foreign companies dislike that Indonesia's military retains "extensive business holdings" and that they must pay for "irregular fees".[59] Nepotism in Indonesia's "awarding of government contracts and concessions" is also a problem.[60] According to Human Rights Watch, there are even worse human rights violations:

> New allegations of security force involvement in torture emerged in 2010. But the military consistently shields its officers from investigations and the government makes little effort to hold them accountable. The government has also done too little to curb discrimination against and attacks on religious, sexual, and ethnic minorities.[61]

This sort of military fascism is a disappointment, especially considering the progress Indonesia has made after decades of authoritarianism in shifting towards a more democratic platform. It is hoped that Indonesia will avoid the mistakes that Burma has made, which have had economic repercussions.

Conclusion

Indonesian law may need to be revised; it is based on a mixture of Roman-Dutch law and indigenous concepts. Existing property rights need to be upheld, corruption needs to be more taken more seriously, and Indonesia should then be able open up to more foreign investment. My socio-political ideas could help Indonesians of all classes, but especially those that are suffering the most.

Laos

The government of Laos, Lao People's Revolutionary Party (LPRP) is very closely aligned with Vietnam's CPV. The LPRP was created in secret in the 1970's and took control as a "strict socialist regime" in 1975.[62]

Undeveloped infrastructure is the most crucial issue facing Laos. The US cluster-bombing of Laos during the end of the Vietnam war has left a deadly legacy—about 80 million unexploded ordnance still lie on Laotian fields.[63] Many have turned to salvaging ordnance for metal parts. So far it is unclear how Laos intends to address this issue.

Human trafficking is also a problem in Laos. From the US Department of State's report on Laos: "Lao men, women, and children are found in conditions of forced labor in Thailand. The government has never administratively or criminally punished any public official for complicity in trafficking in persons."[64]

If left unchecked, the Laotian government has the possibility of becoming as corrupt as Vietnam—this would be disastrous. Steps need to be taken to guide Laos towards a more democratic political system.

Malaysia

Although poverty is still an ongoing concern in Malaysia, economic reforms towards a multi-sector economy have raised its poverty line considerably. Malaysia is, however, a country filled with corruption. Moreover, it is a major hotbed for humans trafficked for the purposes of forced labor. According to the US Department of State's 2010 Report on Human Trafficking:

> The majority of trafficking victims are
> foreign workers who migrate willingly to
> Malaysia from Indonesia, Nepal, India,
> Thailand, China, the Philippines, Burma,
> Cambodia, Bangladesh, Pakistan, and
> Vietnam in search of greater economic
> opportunities, some of whom subsequently
> encounter forced labor or debt bondage at
> the hands of their employers, employment
> agents, or informal labor recruiters.[65]

This is unacceptable—Malaysia's government needs to address human trafficking, especially in regards to forced labor. If Malaysia eliminated internal forced labor, much of the illegal forced labor in all of Southeast Asia would be stifled.

Mongolia

The economy of resource-rich Mongolia is hampered by government corruption. Malnourishment has reached nearly epidemic proportions, however, there is little that can be done to improve Mongolia's situation until systemic corruption and negligence of infrastructure by foreign investors are addressed by Mongolia's government. Mongolia is a candidate for minimal development.

Nepal

Nepal is one of the poorest countries in the world. Despite having a modest reserve of largely unexploited minerals, its economy relies primarily on the textiles industry and agriculture. The country depends heavily on Indian support to bolster its economy—65% of its commercial exports end up in India. Lack of foreign support is affected by political instability caused by the Maoist insurgency in Nepal. After ten years of civil war, a ceasefire was declared in 2006 and an interim constitution was adopted in 2007. Nepal now considers itself a federal democratic republic, although the King still has political influence. Judging by the plurality of communists in power as a result of the Maoist uprising, it seems that Nepal may be doomed to follow in the footsteps of China. Considering that China is interested in investing in Nepal's mineral wealth,[66] the country may just decide to have its own Cultural Revolution.

North Korea

In recent years, North Korea's nuclear weapons program has presented a greater threat in the North Pacific, particularly for South Korea and Japan. North Korea has made international news most notably for its second successful test of a nuclear weapon on May 25, 2009, and the military engagement at Yeonpyeong on November 23, 2010, in which North and South Korea exchanged fire. North Korea's pursuit of military might has come at the expense of its own people, however:

> North Korea, one the world's most centrally directed and least open economies, faces chronic economic problems. Large-scale military spending draws off resources needed for investment and civilian consumption. Industrial and power output have stagnated for years at a fraction of pre-1990 levels.[67]

North Korea scored the lowest possible rank on the Heritage Foundation's Economic Freedom Index for 2011. Despite the promises in North Korea's constitution:

> Property rights are not guaranteed. Almost all property, including nearly all real property, belongs to the state, and the judiciary is not independent. The impoverished population is heavily dependent on food rations and government subsidies in housing, and the state-run rationing system has deteriorated significantly. Deprivation is widespread.[68]

These problems stem from North Korea's socialist "democratic" political system. Not unlike the People's Republic of China, the Democratic People's Republic of Korea (DPRK) is essentially a one-party state, whereby the Workers' Party of Korea (WPK) controls all other political parties, industries, media, and especially the economy. The DPRK's political stranglehold on North Koreans surpasses even that of the PRC; Kim Jong-Il, North Korea's head of state, is a totalitarian dictator whose authority is very nearly absolute. His father, Kim Sung-Il, who led the country as Prime Minister from 1948-1972 and then as President from 1972 until his death in 1994, set up this power paradigm. Although he is dead, North Korean law considers Kim sung-il to be the Eternal President of North Korea; Kim Jong-Il is designated as the Supreme Leader, but does not hold the title of president as a result of this. The concept of Juche is the crucial idea behind Kim Sung-Il's incredible political success and his vast wealth of power.

Juche: North Korea's Political Philosophy

In Kim Sung-Il's immortal words, "Man is the master of everything and decides everything—this is the basis of the Juche idea."[69] In 1972, a new constitution based on Juche was adopted into law. These are the first 3 paragraphs of the preamble to the constitution, unabridged:

> "The Democratic People's Republic of Korea is the socialist motherland of Juche, which has applied the idea and leadership of the great leader Comrade Kim Il Sung.
>
> The great leader Comrade Kim Il Sung is the founder of the Democratic People's Republic of Korea and the father of socialist Korea. Comrade Kim Il Sung authored the immortal Juche idea and, by organizing and leading the anti-Japanese revolutionary struggle under its banner, created the glorious revolutionary traditions and achieved the historic cause of the restoration of national sovereignty.
>
> On the basis of laying a solid foundation for the building of an independent and sovereign State in the political, economic, cultural, and military fields, he founded the Democratic People's Republic of Korea. Having put forward Juche-oriented revolutionary lines, Comrade Kim Il Sung wisely led various stages of social revolution and construction to strengthen and develop the Republic into a socialist country centered on the masses, into a socialist

State which is independent, self-sufficient
and self-reliant in defense."[70]

One of the main goals of the WPK is to reunify Korea
under its socialist banner, which could be brought about
"by carrying out a thorough cultural revolution, training
all the people to be builders of socialism and communism
equipped with a profound knowledge of nature and society
and a high level of culture and technology, thus making
the whole of society intellectual."[71] Although Article 9 of
the constitution suggests that North Korea is peacefully
attempting reunification, recent military conflicts suggest
otherwise. As there is a pretense of peaceful diplomacy
within North Korea's constitution, so too is there also
a pretense of equal rights for its citizens. In theory the
constitution provides these rights, but the political practices
of the WPK are anything but benevolent. The following is a
list of the direst problems facing North Korea:

1. Possibility of a famine epidemic.
2. Trafficking in women.
3. Corrupt prison system and judiciary.
4. Economic isolation.

Possibility of Famine

In the mid 1990's North Korea suffered one of the worst
peacetime famine epidemics wherein an estimated 2 million
people died, mostly due to decreased aid from Russia and
foreign sanctions aimed at demilitarizing the country.[72]
After increased US-backed sanctions in 2002, foreign aid
drastically dropped, and although 2005 saw an increase
in grain production, mostly due to fertilizers provided by

South Korea, the production of 4.5 million tons of grain[73] was still below the 6 million tons as outlined by the World Food Program, and thus inadequate.[74] Furthermore, in this same year, North Korea cut its grain distribution from 300 grams (10.5 oz) of grain per day to just 250 grams (8.8 oz), half of what is required by the World Food Program, and food prices have inflated by 30%. [75] In October 2010, North Korea demanded 500,000 tons of rice and 300,000 tons of fertilizer aid from South Korea in exchange for discussion on regularization of reunion events for separated families.[76]

Trafficking in Women

Women and teenagers who attempt to flee into China from North Korea, or those who are sold into slavery by their family are considered defectors by the government of North Korea,[77] and the Chinese government considers them illegal immigrants.[78] [79] Chinese officials can either imprison them in their own labor camps, or deport them back to North Korea, where they can also be subjected to internment in a labor camp and/or sentenced to execution on the grounds that they are political defectors.[80] Most of the defectors who flee North Korea, including the women who are part of the sex slave trade, do so because of extreme poverty and famine.[81]

Once in China, crooked brokers specializing in human trafficking sell these women, sometimes for only a few hundred dollars, into forced concubine relationships.[82] Many of them are raped and beaten by their new husbands and if they complain they are threatened with deportation back to North Korea.[83] Some of them manage to escape into South Korea, the only safe haven in East Asia.[84] Those that do not either remain sex slaves in China, or are deported back into North Korea and imprisoned in labor camps, where conditions are just as inhumane as the Chinese Laogai prison camps.

Prison System

Kwan-li-so is a "series of sprawling encampments" in the northern provinces of North Korea—there are an estimated 150,000-200,000 prisoners in these camps.[85] According to Tennessee politician and human rights expert David Hawk: "The long-term imprisonment and short-term detention facilities are both characterized by below-subsistence-level food rations and very high levels of deaths in detention."[86] Not unlike the Chinese prisons, there is high incidence of beatings, posture torture, and water torture.[87]

Shin Dong-Hyuk, a Camp 14 survivor and its only known escapee, wrote a book in which he describes the rape and beatings of imprisoned relatives, his own gruesome torture, and the murder of his mother.[88] Shin's tale is unusual, not only because he escaped, but also because his birth in prison went unpunished—most infants born in kwan-li-so prison camps are forcibly aborted, often by having their necks crushed.[89] These infanticides "are the direct result of KIM Il Sung's dictates: 'Factionalists or enemies of class, whoever they are, their seed must be eliminated through three generations.' Accordingly, pregnancy and childbirth are considered as crimes and those involved are cruelly punished and executed along with their babies."[90]

Camp 22, one of the largest kwan-li-so camps, houses gas chambers where chemical experiments are carried out on prisoners. From an article in The Observer: "Witnesses have described watching entire families being put in glass chambers and gassed. They are left to an agonizing death while scientists take notes."[91]

Public executions

After a brief decline in the early 2000's, public execution made a comeback in 2007. For instance, in October 2007, "a factory chief accused of making international phone calls was shot down at a stadium before a crowd of 150,000 people"[92], and in 2008, 15 people were publicly executed in the town of Onseong for illegally attempting to cross the border into China.[93] What's worse is that children are allowed to attend such events. For instance, one testimony describes a class trip "to attend a public execution near the school. The DPRK bound the heads, necks, breasts, abdomens, and legs of three persons to pillars. Each person was shot three times. Brain parts splattered onto the children in the front row. There have been numerous other eye witness accounts of children forced to attend public executions."[94] The DPRK's wish to instill fear into the populace using public executions is quite transparent, and is condemned by the UN General Assembly.[95]

Economic Isolation

North Korea's economy is still largely planned and controlled by the central government, which makes "entrepreneurial activity . . . virtually impossible".[96] Reliable financial statistics are very hard to come by for North Korea:

> North Korea stopped publishing economic statistics as long ago as the 1960s, when

its rapid early growth began to slow. The government's tendency to view policies through the lens of Marxist thought, ignoring the crucial role played by the limited (and often illicit) private sector, results in serious errors in monetary policy. In theory, most prices are regulated by the state, but food is the main budget item for most North Koreans, so domestic agricultural production dictates underlying consumer price inflation. Volatility in the size of harvests is likely. Consequently, periods of very high inflation are possible.[97]

Conclusion

Corruption is the greatest obstacle to economic freedom in North Korea. The DPRK's obstinacy in regulating nearly all aspects of its economy 100% has only hindered economic and human development. Given the nature of my economic revolution, very high inflation in food prices will no longer have a negative impact on the people of North Korea. That being said, other political and economic issues must be addressed.

Although most of the forced laborers are legitimately imprisoned for crimes that would be considered felonies in the US,[98] North Korea needs to reform its prison system. The imprisonment of women in these camps, and the inhumane conditions to which they are subjected is unacceptable, and should be addressed immediately by China and North Korea. Gas chambers are a waste of money and resources—this inhumane practice must be abandoned as well. According to Wall Street: "Numerous countries employ sanctions against

North Korea, and ongoing political and security concerns make investment extremely hazardous."[99] In short, if North Korea's economy is to improve, the DPRK should:

1. Reform the prison system and the judiciary.
2. Publish more economic statistics for North Korea.
3. Establish new trade partners.
4. Allow for minimal private sector investment.

This 4 point plan will jumpstart North Korea's economy while still allowing the DPRK to consolidate power through regulations.

Philippines

Money laundering is the number one problem in the Philippines:

> The principle sources of criminal proceeds are human and drug trafficking, official corruption, and investment scams. The Philippines' geographic position makes it attractive to human and narcotics traffickers; and relatively open sea borders complicate enforcement of currency controls. The Philippines continues to experience an increase in foreign organized criminal activity from China, Hong Kong, and Taiwan. Insurgency groups operating in the Philippines partially fund their activities through local crime and the trafficking of narcotics and arms, and engage in money laundering through ties to organized crime.

> Smuggling, including bulk cash smuggling,
> continues to be a problem.[100]

Unfortunately, poverty worsened in 2010. Until pervasive and endemic corruption is rooted out, specifically in the sphere of money laundering, the Philippines will continue to be a poor country with poor human rights.

Sri Lanka

Sri Lanka, a low-income country, "depends heavily on foreign assistance, and China has become a significant lender for infrastructure projects."[101] Terrorism has recently been eradicated in Sri Lanka:

> In April 2010, President Mahinda
> Rajapakse's ruling coalition won a
> landslide victory in parliamentary elections.
> Rajapakse's re-election was attributed to
> his government's success in defeating the
> terrorist Liberation Tigers of Tamil Eelam
> (LTTE) and eliminating its top leadership
> in 2009, thus ending a three-decade civil
> war that took the lives of some 70,000
> people.[102]

As a result of three decades of civil war, corruption has become endemic in Sri Lanka:

> Anti-corruption laws and regulations
> are unevenly enforced. The police and
> judiciary are viewed as the most corrupt
> public institutions. Corruption in customs

clearance enables wide-scale smuggling of certain consumer items. In 2008, the Supreme Court removed the Secretary to the Treasury from his position and ruled that he may not hold any public office in the future.[103]

Corruption is the greatest obstacle to economic improvement in Sri Lanka. The recent parliamentary victories are a hopeful sign that problems of corruption in Sri Lanka will be significantly reduced in the near future.

Thailand

Thailand, a constitutional monarchy, managed to avoid the mistake of communism, yet it suffers from similar corruption problems to those that exist in most of Southeast Asia, such as contract kickbacks for politicians and policemen.[104] Its free-market economy is fairly solid, but it needs to root out extensive corruption in the public sector.

Vietnam

At the conclusion of the Vietnamese war, the Northern government unified the country under Communist rule. With the establishment of "doi moi" policy in 1986, the Socialist Republic of Vietnam liberalized its economy by modernizing industry and focusing on export commodities. Despite economic advances, there are still problems with widespread corruption and poverty. 10-19% of Vietnam's population of 90 million is affected by malnourishment.[105]

Censorship and Human Rights Violations

Under the rule of the Communist Party of Vietnam (CPV), Vietnamese suffer similar censorship and restrictions as occur in China and North Korea. Things have only gotten worse in recent years—in 2009, the CPV intensified its suppression of dissidents by imprisoning and torturing some of them.[106] According to Human Rights Watch:

> The government tightened its controls on internet use, blogging, and independent research, and banned dissemination and publication of content critical of the government. Religious freedom continued to deteriorate, with the government targeting religious leaders and their followers who advocated for civil rights, religious freedom, and equitable resolution of land disputes.[107]

First of all, one must understand that the CPV is cracking down on religious expression because it is obsessed with maintaining complete control. Although their methods of repression are deplorable, it is important that there is still separation of church and state.

Property rights are lacking in Vietnam: "Only the rudiments of a system to protect property rights have been established. The judiciary is not independent, and corruption is common. Contracts are weakly enforced, and resolution of disputes can take years. Infringement of property rights is also common."[108] In 2010, "Public protests over evictions, confiscation of church properties, and police brutality were met at times with excessive use of force by police. Police routinely tortured suspects in custody."[109]

Conclusion

My political-economic plan could win over the support of Vietnam's government, because it represents a compromise between socialism and democracy that would be very appealing to the CPV. Every country is different and will approach my ideas differently. In the case of Vietnam, I fully support government regulations of big business. The state should not feel pressured by other nations of the world who disagree with this method of business conduct; however, it is vital for Vietnam to promise to increase transparency and provide accountability for revenues.

Vietnam's real growth has been solid in the past few years despite the global economic crisis. If, however, the CPV expects future economic growth, Vietnam must compromise by allowing for more private sector business growth. At the moment, foreign investment in Vietnam is either prohibited or at the very least requires government approval.[110] While the latter agrees with my socialist leanings, the former is a problem since it only serves to hinder Vietnam from growing economically. Vietnam needs to open up to foreign investment outside of the Association of Southeast Asian Nations (ASEAN), which will only happen if Vietnam compromises by allowing for more private sector growth. Also important is for Vietnam to address property rights issues. 100% state ownership of land is prevents foreign investment in Vietnam.

Vietnam's main political-economic goals are:

1. Allow foreign ownership of a small percentage of land.
2. Allow for private sector growth.
3. Amend the constitution.
4. End proscription of opposition parties.
5. Improve property right laws.
6. Create an independent judiciary.
7. Protect human rights.

By addressing these seven issues, Vietnam will gain the trust and support of nations outside of the Asian bloc, repair its infrastructure and create a more sustainable economy. Needless to say, my socioeconomic reform will benefit all Vietnamese.

Conclusion

Corruption and poverty plague most of Asia. Communism is still very much alive in Asia, and the resultant lack of human rights that accompany it are to be deplored. Nevertheless, the political system has thus far served China economically, and, since the fall of the Soviet Union, slight improvements in human rights have been made in most of the Communist countries of Asia. My advice to all of these nations is to look to Russia as a political-economic model to follow.

Chapter 3

Africa

Even if my socioeconomic theory were implemented worldwide, Human Development would still be an ongoing concern, particularly for Africa. Nevertheless, the categories of Human Development will gradually need to be reassessed. In general, African countries that are heavily dependent on agriculture fall into two categories, those that are maximizing human development and those that are perpetually entrapped in minimal human development.

Minimal Human Development

These are primarily Heavily Indebted Poor Countries who rely almost exclusively on international aid to subsist. These countries are characterized by high activity in the agricultural sector and high unemployment. In light of my anti-authoritarian views on politics, I believe that the wishes of indigenous people must be respected. Many of the "unemployed" in Africa are actually working, but their work does not contribute to the GDP of their respective nations. As a result, many impoverished subsistence farmers and nomadic herdspeople remain impoverished, for instance, in Djibouti. It would not be right to deprive these people of their right to remain minimally developed, as this would constitute extreme political authoritarianism. Examples of the negative effects of this kind of authoritarianism can be seen throughout Asia where human rights abuses are prolific. Furthermore, despite authoritarianism and a demand to increase industry in Asia, malnourishment and poverty have persisted. Therefore I am arguing to maintain the paradigm of international foreign assistance for countries that are minimally developed.

The goal, however, is to mirror similar successes in other developed nations, such as South Africa, and to learn from the mistakes of less developed nations. Although improved industry is a must, rapid industrialization is to be discouraged. Despite the fact that the Cultural Revolution pushed China into the forefront of the world economy in regards to industry, chronic rural poverty has persisted because industrialization was pursued too quickly—thus it remains a country of medium human development. China is, by the way, the greatest example of this mistake. Therefore, minimal improvements in the industrialization of agriculture and mining should be pursued in many of Africa's poorest nations in order to achieve economic success.

Free Medicine

If my socioeconomic theory were to be implemented in Africa, free medicine distribution to countries in Africa that suffer from high risk of disease would be limited only by existing supply.

Conclusion

There will still be poverty in Africa despite socioeconomic reform, and basic infrastructure improvements must occur slowly if Asia's mistakes are to be avoided. Although the alleviation of suffering in Africa will contribute to an overall increase in the score for well-being in low-development countries, certain countries may still not rise into the ranks of medium human development, due to minimal industrial progress. These countries must be considered minimal human development countries. The crucial idea is that minimal development balances the difficult task of creating a sustainable society while simultaneously respecting the rights of its indigenous populace.

Angola

Angola is war-torn country whose struggle for independence from the Portuguese caused a civil war between two extreme-left political groups that spanned three decades, leading to massive corruption in its government and widespread rural poverty. Although not as intense, the destructive aftermath of Angola's decades long civil war mirrors the situation in the Democratic Republic of Congo—it has caused the displacement of some 4 million people, and has led to massive poverty and famine.[111] The landmines and unexploded bombs that litter the countryside are a danger to those who want to return and cultivate the land,[112] leaving only 2% of rural land available for cultivation.[113] This is a severe problem for the majority of Angolans who depend on subsistence agriculture for their very survival:[114]

Poverty is far more severe and widespread in rural areas, where an estimated 94 per cent of households are poor. Although the war ended in 2002, conditions remain extremely difficult. Housing is rudimentary and health services cover only 30 per cent of rural areas. The majority of households have no electricity and no adequate sanitation. Access to safe drinking water is also limited, and more than 60 per cent of rural households obtain their water from unsafe sources.[115]

Corruption

According to Transparency International's 2009 corruption index, Angola ranked among the world's 18 most corrupt countries.[116] In 2010, the Human Rights Watch published an excellent report on the subject. Its summary of Angola's corruption is as follows:

> The government of Jose Eduardo dos Santos, in power in Angola since 1979, has historically mismanaged the country's substantial oil revenues and used its control over oil wealth to insulate itself from public scrutiny. Angola remains an example of the problems that plague a resource-rich state. It relies on a centrally controlled major revenue stream and is therefore not reliant on domestic taxation or a diversified economy to function. Its rulers have unique opportunities for self-enrichment and corruption, especially because there is not enough transparency or political space for the public to hold them accountable. There

are enormous disincentives to relinquish political power because it is also a path to economic enrichment. It is no accident that the president of Angola, one of the world's major oil producers, is entering his fourth decade in power.[117]

There are several key players in past corruption who had much to gain by keeping the state budget a secret, namely Pierre Falcone, an arms dealer closely associated with President dos Santos, and Dr. Aguinaldo Jaime, who served as governor of the Angolan Central Bank from 1999-2002.[118] Falcone brokered an arms-for-oil deal with the Angolan government in the early 1990s to the tune of $600 million worth of weapons. These weapons purchases were paid for with Angolan proceeds from Sonangol oil sales.[119] Jaime is suspected of embezzling $50 million dollars by transferring the money to several different banks on multiple occasions.[120] During Jaime's three-year tenure, the Angolan government couldn't account for approximately $2.4 billion.[121]

China's Involvement

Not surprisingly, China has some involvement in Angola's corrupt government. The China International Fund (CIF) provided approximately $2.9 billion to Angola via the Reconstruction Office of Angola (GRN) and formed a joint-venture with Sonangol called China Sonangol International Holding, Limited (CSIH).[122] According to a public statement, the CIF, a Hong Kong based company, is completely autonomous from Chinese government, and reports directly to the Angolan presidency.[123] As a result,

Ethan James

there is no need for the company to account for transactions of funds, and given the secrecy of China's government, it's quite possible that they do not audit the CIF.

There is only one tenuous link between the CIF and Angola's corrupt government. In 2006, the Head of the External Intelligence Service, General Fernando Miala was dismissed from office and charged with insubordination. During his trial, he threatened to identify senior Angolan officials who benefited from illegal trade with the CIF.[124] Although he was imprisoned, Miala was pardoned and released in 2009, but it wouldn't be a surprise if he finally revealed certain guilty parties in the future.

There are several solutions being discussed in order to reduce the possibility of corruption in business agreements between Angola and the CIF. The IMF (International Monetary Fund) has struck deals with the Angolan government in order to persuade it to provide transparency in its oil transactions, but the government has not provided a full audit as of yet. The Human Rights Watch issued several suggestions to China's government:

1. Full disclosure of the CIF's relationship to China's government.
2. Full disclosure of the CIF's business interests with Sonangol.
3. Full disclosure of the CIF's global holdings, revenues, and audit expenditures.[125]

Conclusion

According to the United Nations Development Program, "The reduction of poverty, particularly of extreme poverty, continues to be a priority for the Angolan State and the development stakeholders in the country."[126] Progress is slowly being made by the UNDP, such as the creation of 117 new jobs, and some advances in combating the AIDS epidemic in Angola, but the UNDP didn't meet all of its 2009 goals.[127] Until the government of Angola becomes more cooperative with international groups such as the UNDP and the IMF, it is unlikely that all of their goals will ever be reached. There are several key criticisms of China's involvement with Angola:

> The rise of China as Angola's main trading partner has helped the Angolan government resist reforms, not least because China and Chinese companies do not call for good governance. China is the world's largest importer of Angolan oil [36% share][128] and Angola is China's largest trading partner in Africa. The Chinese government's economic influence as a key trading partner is substantial, but it has avoided discussing governance or transparency, helping to slow Angola's path towards accountability.[129]

Corruption prevents Angola from developing its infrastructure. Oil production provides the country with 85% of its GDP[130], yet Angola's government has not provided impoverished subsistence farmers with the most essential of resources. Fortunately, my revolution will resolve the latter problem. As for China's involvement, it is hoped that the country will eventually help build infrastructure as they have with other African countries, and work with Angola's government to improve human rights.

Burundi

Burundi is a Hutu majority nation. The assassination of Burundi's first Hutu president, Melchior Ndadaye, "sparked" a civil war in 1993[131] and ultimately led to the Rwandan genocide in 1994. Although there is officially peace between Hutus and Tutsis, the country still suffers from corruption and political violence, despite a democratic constitution in 2005. Government corruption is an obstacle to fixing the various problems in Burundi, such as high unemployment, endemic poverty, and shortages of food, medicine, and electricity (less than 2% of the population has electricity in its homes).[132] As of 2011, widespread malnourishment is an epidemic affecting 20-34% of the population. [133]

Human Rights Violations and Political Violence

The 2010 elections were preceded by much violence: "Before and throughout the elections most major parties used intimidation tactics, including violence."[134] Although many were involved, the chief instigator of violence was the majority party, National Council for the Defense of Democracy-Forces for the Defense of Democracy. Brutal, authoritarian tactics were employed by the CNDD-FDD in order to win the elections:

> Government officials banned opposition meetings and tortured political opponents.

> In the two weeks before communal
> elections at least five politically-motivated
> killings took place. During the presidential
> and legislative elections at least 128
> grenade attacks—many of them targeting
> political activists on all sides—took place
> throughout Burundi, killing 11 and injuring
> at least 69.[135]

In addition to accusations of electoral fraud in the
majority win by CNDD-FDD, corruption is "pervasive" all
across the board in the government of Burundi:

> From senior government officials demanding
> large kickbacks on procurement tenders to
> low-level civil servants demanding petty
> bribes for services, licenses, or permits,
> corruption is present in every area of
> life. It is most pervasive in government
> procurement, where the purchase and sale
> of government property frequently leads to
> allegations of bribery and cronyism.[136]

Burundi's government does not protect the right to
private property, which has negative consequences for
people still displaced by the civil war:

> Private property is subject to government
> expropriation and armed banditry. The
> constitution guarantees the independence
> of the judiciary, but judges are appointed
> by the executive branch and are subject
> to political pressure. A large number of

> refugees and internally displaced persons are blocked from resettlement by weak land tenure and property rights systems and by the lack of ownership records.[137]

Business in Burundi is inefficient as a result of stiff regulations and instability caused by corruption, both of which inhibit entrepreneurial activity.[138] It is very rich in unexploited mineral reserves, however, until political instability is resolved, the country will continue to have an "underdeveloped financial sector" providing a "very limited range of services."[139] Consequently, the country will remain poor until it becomes more politically stable.

Conclusion

The need for Burundi to develop a sustainable economy is, first and foremost, geographically determined—it is landlocked and surrounded by states with similar political unrest, which makes it very difficult for foreign nations to safely intervene on its behalf. The first step is to achieve political stability. I believe that Burundians should place their trust in the Front for Democracy in Burundi, since its goals are socialist. This group can help Burundi achieve a more stable economy and alleviate poverty, which, in turn, will ease tensions between Hutus and Tutsis.

Cameroon

Nearly 40% of Cameroon's population lives on $1.25 per day and agriculture accounts for 70% of Cameroon's labor force. The risk of infectious disease is very high. Like Angola, Cameroon is a corrupt oil country. Transparency of oil-related revenue needs improvement as economic mismanagement continues to impede human development.[140] There are, however, many other obstacles to freedom in Cameroon:

> Three major banks still dominate the banking sector, and the sector's performance has deteriorated due to lack of transparency and accountability in lending. Property rights Courts and government agencies have been accused of corrupt practices, and there continue to be reports of beatings of detainees, arbitrary arrests, and illegal searches. Despite anti-corruption and good-governance initiatives, legal loopholes and legislative gaps allowing corruption have not been eliminated. Corruption and legal uncertainty can lead to confiscation of private property. Courts and administrative agencies often favor domestic firms and are accused of corruption. Some foreign companies allege that unfavorable judgments are the result of fraud or frivolous lawsuits. Corruption, cumbersome bureaucracy, and decision-making delays persist.[141]

Considering the government's outright corruption and neglect of human rights, it is not surprising that forced labor is endemic in Cameroon as well:

> A 2007 study conducted by the Cameroon government reported that 2.4 million

children from the country's ten regions involuntarily work in forced domestic servitude, street vending, and child prostitution, or in hazardous settings, including mines and tea or cocoa plantations, where they are treated as adult laborers; an unknown number of these children are trafficking victims. Nigerian and Beninese children attempting to transit Cameroon en route to Gabon, Equatorial Guinea, or adjacent countries also fall into the hands of traffickers who force them to stay in the country and work.[142]

Paul Biya has held office as president since 1982; he has further consolidated his power as the authoritarian head of state:

In 2008, Biya's supporters in parliament, having won a strong majority in 2007, passed constitutional amendments granting the president immunity for acts committed while in office and enabling Biya to run yet again in 2011. Public frustration with poor governance threatens to spark political unrest.[143]

Conclusion

Although the IMF has called for reform, little has been done to comply with their requests. There are several solutions to improving the average Cameroonian's quality of life. For starters, my socioeconomic theory could help to alleviate some endemic malnourishment. The Social Democratic Front also needs to play a larger role in Cameroon's government in order to more effectively challenge Biya's control of the country.

Chad

After 3 decades civil war and conflict, relative peace has been achieved in oil-rich Chad. Although there is political instability caused by ongoing conflict between the government of Chad and Sudanese rebels, corruption within the government of Chad continues to remain the greatest obstacle to economic sustainability and the relief of humanitarian crises in Chad. According to the Heritage Foundation:

> Despite a "Ministry of Morality" that conducts anti-corruption seminars for government employees, corruption exists at all levels of government. It may be most pervasive in the customs and tax enforcement services, but it is notable in the judiciary and government procurement as well. The government actively obstructs the work of domestic human rights organizations through arrest, detention, and intimidation.[144]

Crises and Economic Injustices

Famine is endemic, affecting up to 35% of the population.[145] Human Rights groups have deplored the use of children in forced labor as herders, domestic servants, agricultural laborers, or beggars.[146] Additionally, property rights are compromised by corruption in the judiciary, many judicial authorities are "subject to political influence".[147] Business in the "private-sector development" is hampered by "inefficient and unstructured regulatory system".[148]

Conclusion

Chad is a landlocked country, which has made foreign assistance difficult. Movement towards a sustainable society must start with the leaders of Chad, who could benefit greatly from many of the political-economical ideas I've presented in this book. Above all, anti-corruption measures need improvement so as to crackdown on government corruption.

Côte d'Ivoire

Côte d'Ivoire is in the midst of a civil war that could very well result in two separate countries. Due to political instability and corruption in Côte d'Ivoire, it may be years before economic improvements can be made. My two cents is that Côte d'Ivoire should remain unified; succession has led to many political disasters throughout history, such as the succession of North Korea from South Korea.

The Democratic Republic of Congo

The political ripples of the Rwandan Genocide (1994) contributed to The First Congo War (1996-1997), which started as a result of Rwandan refugees, Congolese rebels, and the Congolese army fighting for control of mineral resources. For instance, the goal of the Banyamulenge

Rebellion was to seize control of the eastern Kivu province, an area rich with copper and gold. The rebellion was fomented by Laurent Kabila, who formed the Alliance of Democratic Forces for Liberation of Congo (ADFL) in order to topple the existing regime. In 1997, president Mobutu Sese Seko died, and after a series of military victories, Kabila succeeded him as president of Zaire, which was renamed The Democratic Republic of the Congo.

The Second Congo War (1998-2003) was the deadliest conflict since WWII—some 5 million people perished, mostly as a result of disease and starvation.[149] Millions were displaced either within the Congo or within other nearby countries.[150] Although the war ended in 2003, the conflicts in the Congo have not ended—famine and disease are currently claiming Congolese at a rate of 45,000 per month.[151] There are currently 1500 war related deaths per day.[152] That's 547,500 deaths per year, about 5 times more than all of the civilian casualties between 2003-2011 in the Iraq War[153]. 71% of the Congo's population lives below the poverty line and the per capita GDP was an astonishing $300 in 2010.[154] The Congo is one of the poorest countries in the world.

The Ongoing Conflict

Many of the same conflicts that started the war are still playing out to this very day in the provinces of Ituri, and North and South Kivu. The central power struggle is between the FDLR (The Democratic Forces for the Liberation of Rwanda) and the FARDC (The Armed Forces of the Democratic Republic of Congo). Meanwhile, MONUSCO (The United Nations Organization Stabilization Mission of The Democratic Republic of the Congo), passed by

Resolution 1925 in May 2010, continues its peacekeeping mission. The UN has had a lasting presence in the Congo; its first operations took place during the Second Congo War. The UN's mission name has changed as many times as its mission has changed, in order to accommodate the ever-forming political rifts in the Congo.

Both the FARDC and the FDLR oppose other political groups that splintered off from the CNDP (National Congress for the Defense of the People) and the RCD (The Rally for Congolese Democracy). Even though the CNDP became a political party after its former leader, Laurent Nkunda, was arrested in January 2009, it still poses a military threat should relations between the CNDP and the FADRC falter. Because, or despite of these new political rifts in recent years, the UN has continued to monitor closely the actions of the FDLR and other rebel groups. The FDLR is still attempting to annex the Ituri and Kivu provinces because they are mineral rich resources; this is understandable because Rwanda's economy is based almost entirely upon agriculture. As a result of this power struggle, and the heinous nature of the Hutu Power philosophy, many war crimes are still being committed in the Eastern Congo.

For instance, In August 2010, Mai Mai militiamen and Hutus belonging to the FDLR systematically gang-raped 200 Congolese women near a UN base in Luvungi, a farming town in North Kivu.[155] In October 2010, UN peacekeepers repelled a Mai Mai militia attack on their base in Rwindi, North Kivu, killing 8 rebels.[156] There is still the possibility of a renewed conflict on the scale of the 2009 Eastern Congo Offensive, in which thousands of FDLR rebels were repelled by the combined airstrikes of the Congolese and Rwandan military near Goma, North Kivu, which resulted in the death of a least 40 of the Hutu rebels. While it is encouraging that the FDLR is being put down, it is also troubling that new criminal activities are transpiring.

> According to the Global Witness, "former rebels from the CNDP have established mafia-style extortion rackets covering some of the most lucrative tin and tantalum mining areas in the eastern DRC. 'The ex-CNDP rebels, who joined the national army in a chaotic integration process during 2009, have taken advantage of UN-backed government offensives aimed at displacing the FDLR militia from profitable mine sites. They have gained far greater control of mining areas than they ever enjoyed as insurgents, and in many cases have retained their old command structures and political agenda'.[157]

Corruption is the cause of all of these conflicts—perhaps it was unwise for the FADRC to absorb rebels from the CNDP into its ranks in the first place. Needless to say, violence will continue indefinitely in the Eastern Congo as long as mafia-style corruption is allowed to persist.

The Chinese Connection

During the Second Congo War, one of the most important mineral resources was coltan, a dull, black mineral found almost exclusively in the conflict regions of eastern Congo. Tantalum is extracted from coltan and is necessary to build the capacitors used for electronics equipment such as cellphones, computers, and videogame systems. Not only is the Congo still rich in these resources, it also has the other necessary ores to produce electronic equipment, such as copper (for wires) and cassiterite, the only reliable source of tin, one of the metals least prone to oxidization, which is used to coat chips and other metal parts in order to prevent oxidization.

China's involvement with DRC's coltan trade took off in 1999 with the formation of Ningxia Orient Tantalum Industry Corporation Limited (OTIC), in order to facilitate distribution of its tantalum, produced by its mining and smelting company, Ningxia Non-Ferrous Metals Smeltery (NNMS). OTIC supplies processed tantalum to companies such as Kemet, Vishay, Hitachi, and NEC—all of the biggest names in capacitor production. These companies supply capacitors to circuit board producers, and the finished products end up being marketed and sold by companies such as Dell, Nokia, HP, IBM, and the former Motorola, Inc.[158] What's interesting is that coltan mining in DRC increased exponentially after the creation of OTIC; in 1999, mining output was negligible, yet in 2000, 130 metric tons of ore were mined in DRC, contributing to 12% of the world's mined coltan.[159] For the next ten years, there was a dropoff and stabilization in the amount of Coltan mined from DRC. Information about OTIC is extremely difficult to come by, but reliable statistics show that the company assets are currently over $235 million.[160]

Chinese mining practices in the Congo border on the inhumane. According to a company report,[161] the main problems are as follows:

1. Chinese companies do not understand nor do they follow neither the Congolese Code du Travail nor international labor laws.

2. Environmental standards are not respected.
3. Accidents in Chinese-run smelters are commonplace because workers do not wear protective gear, nor are they taught safety procedures.
4. Medical compensation for serious injuries is often inadequate or non-existent.
5. Use of illegal child labor.
6. Workers are exposed to radioactive dust.
7. Chinese and Congolese security guards often assault unruly employees.
8. Congolese workers are discriminated against, and there is little room to advance.[162]

Chinese mining companies' poor practices extend well beyond the Congo. In 2008, Bloomberg.com published an article called "China Lets Child Workers Die Digging in Congo Mines for Copper". According to this article, hundreds of workers for Chinese companies have died in Africa, Asia, and Latin America.[163] The article also details how these child laborers are exposed to poisonous—potentially lethal—mineral dust as they crawl around in mine shafts that are prone to collapse because they do not have proper bracing. In the meantime, China has tried to improve relations with Congolese government:

> China expanded its ties with Congo by promising to finance $9 billion of roads, railways and mines in exchange for 10 million metric tons of copper and 600,000 tons of cobalt from six Gecamines-run mines over a decade at a fixed price. China's promises, however, are meaningless to Mbayo Muyambo, who says he's witnessed

> a torrent of injuries as safety director at
> Chinese—controlled Feza Mining Sprl in
> Likasi. Muyambo, says Feza's workers are
> routinely burned at the company's smelter
> by fiery drops of molten cobalt because the
> company doesn't supply fireproof suits.[164]

While it is positive that China is making large investments in Congo's infrastructure, clearly there need to be improvements in the quality of its work environments and better adherence to international labor laws. The Bloomberg article ended on a promising note: "In an effort to bridge the growing chasm between rich and poor and to close down the worst sweat shops, Chinese President Hu passed new labor laws setting minimum wages and assuring one month's pay for each year worked for employees who get fired"[165]. There is no new evidence to suggest that the working conditions are any safer, therefore one must conclude that China's companies are still operating in violation of International Labor Organization law.

The Illegal Gold Trade

In February, 2.5 tons of gold worth about $113 million was transported out of the Congo.[166] Interpol was contacted to investigate the illegal trading routes. Their investigation found that "consignment of gold stolen from the Democratic Republic of Congo (DRC) have unearthed suspected smuggling syndicates in the middle-East and South Africa, signaling wider and sustained threats to economic and social stability in mineral rich nations in the region."[167] The irony is that there is endemic corruption and illegal gold mining within the Congo; if the country were to crack down on this problem it would be less likely for gold to be smuggled out of the country.

FDLR (Hutu) rebels have been controlling illegal gold mining for over a decade in Eastern Congo, particularly in North and South Kivu.[168] This has been enabled by systemic corruption at all levels of government. Both the Congo's military and the FADRC are working in conjunction with rebel-controlled mines.[169] [170] Furthermore, there are reports of FADRC's soldiers selling weapons and uniforms to the FDLR.[171] "Whilst the activity is largely illegal, clandestine, dangerous, exploitative and fails to return official revenues to the state; it is still the economic backbone of the region generating direct employment for many people".[172] This corrupt paradigm is doomed to become cemented by the ever-increasing involvement of multinational corporations.

The Diamond Trade

The diamond trade in DRC, operated by MIBA (Societé minierè de Bakwanga) is probably the country's most corrupt mineral trade, and although they have been cooperating with the Kimberly Process Certification Scheme in recent years, as much as a third of its diamond resources are still illegally smuggled out of the country each year.[173] In addition, work conditions are poor in the MIBA mines; Mbuji Mayi, the city around which the diamond trade was built "could be described as a small-scale war between the artisanal miners, MIBA, the police, and the suicidaires—named for their suicidal propensity to confront police in shootouts[174]—over access and control of the key diamondiferous areas".[175] As of 2007, many children have worked illegally on the MIBA concessions under the forced control of the suicidaires, and there are many armed fights over the most lucrative areas.[176] In particular, the Polygon, MIBA's largest mining concession, is a veritable war zone.

> Since the liberalization of informal diamond digging in 1982, illegal diggers invade the concession each day, paying an access fee to get through the two belts of security, namely the police and the FADRC. Illegal diggers face several permanent obstacles, which are: at the entry point to the site, they have to pay an access fee of 200 CF per belt of security; reprisal and attacks by the mining guards, police and 'the suicidal'; the deep shafts, the abandoned mines filled with stagnant water, and flash floods in the river during the rainy season; stray bullets fired by the mining police to dissuade illegal diggers and suicidaires. In the face of this plethora of different categories of diggers who enter the MIBA polygon illegally, there is so much confusion that you can't tell who is doing the shooting.[177]

The Congolese government owns roughly 80% of MIBA's stock; the other 20% is owned by Sibeka-Umicore, a Belgian based multinational materials technology whose purpose is to refine and manage precious minerals. Considering that MIBA is worth tens of millions of dollars (although the exact figure is difficult to come by), it is shameful that alluvial diamond miners, digging on their hands and knees, are paid an average of $1 per day. Many of the Congolese believe that their government is embezzling diamond money. Considering the nature of the Polygon's security, this is not necessarily untrue.

For instance, in 2009, tens of thousands of Congolese refugees were caught and detained near the border of neighboring country Angola.[178] Tensions erupted when "miners from the Congo were reportedly beaten and raped after the government of Angola discovered them smuggling in diamonds and mining on foreign soil."[179] A total of 200,000 illegal Congolese miners have been deported back to DRC.[180] Undoubtedly, Joseph Kabila's government is cracking down on some of the suicidaires and illegal smugglers, but until corruption is completely rooted out there will still be illegal diamond smuggling out of DRC.

Illegal smuggling notwithstanding, the working conditions in the mines are pitiful, and rank as a humanitarian crisis. The mining age bracket is 6-45 years of age, and the miners are usually crippled by debt as a result of heavy taxation.[181] Since the diggers are so poor, they generally eat only one meal per day and in some cases, diggers drink the water from the rivers and streams where they sieve and clean stones.[182] This accounts for much of the malnourishment and waterborne illness in the mining communities. International health and safety conditions as outlined by the International Labor Organization are often not followed at all in the artisanal mining sector.[183] Various Codes have been created to protect miners, yet, regrettably:

> Neither the existing *Code Minier* (2002), nor the *Code de Conduite de l'Exploitant Artisanal* (2003), nor the *Plan Minier* (2006) are appropriate or sympathetic to the current realities of the [artisanal mining] sector,

provide no real incentives for legalisation,
and are plagued by contradictions and
unenforceable articles. The Government
lacks the technical capacity and resources to
manage the system, and does not fulfill any
of their legal labour, social or environmental
obligations. Parastatal management systems
are largely incompetent and their integrity
is compromised by endemic corruption.
Significant institutional strengthening,
capacity building, sensitisation and
effective decentralisation is needed to turn
this around".[184]

Conclusion

The government of the Congo needs to provide greater
accountability for revenues. MIBA needs to improve its
miners' rights, and more thoroughly enforce its various work
codes if Chinese mining companies such as Dong Bang
Mining are ever to enforce the Code du Travail. President
Kabila has taken steps to eliminate smuggling, which will
improve Congo's economy.

Ethiopia

Ethiopia's financial system and judiciary remain
underdeveloped.[185] Corruption is rampant in Ethiopia:

Despite legal restrictions, officials have
been accused of manipulating privatization,
and state-owned and party-owned
businesses receive preferential access to

land leases and credit. The Federal Ethics
and Anti-Corruption Commission arrested
or conducted investigations of 203 suspects
from August 2008 to January 2009.[186]

Until corruption is reduced, Ethiopia will remain poor.

Kenya

Kenya is in a country in political transition and represents an extreme humanitarian crisis. Approximately 1.5 million people (6% of its population) are infected with HIV and the birth rate is very high—about 4 children are born to each woman. Unemployment is at 40%. Kenya suffers from pervasive government corruption, which "has led to foreign disinvestment and has drained resources needed for education, health, and infrastructure."[187] The total percentage of the population living below the poverty line is 46%, admittedly a decline from previous years, but a crisis that must be dealt with, especially considering that government corruption and poverty were two of the problems that Kalenjin rebels cited as motivation[188] for targeted post election violence in 2008, which resulted in the deaths of hundreds of Kikuyus.

Mining in Kenya

Kenya has some mineral wealth. According to a 2007 report, "The mining and quarrying sector makes a negligible contribution to the economy, accounting for less than 1 percent of gross domestic product, the majority contributed by the soda ash operation at Lake Magadi in south-central Kenya."[189] What the report neglected to mention is that there is also small-scale mining of very valuable gemstones in Nairobi mines. The 2009 machete assassination of Scottish gem-mining expert Campbell Bridges by illegal miners brought to light the illegal gem mining trade in Nairobi.[190] There are some legal mining companies in the area, but there are also many cartels conducting small-scale mining, very similar to the situation in the Democratic Republic of Congo. In the Congo, crooked security forces allow illegal mining to persist through bribery. A similar scenario would seem to be likely in Kenya considering that graft and money laundering are so prevalent.

One long-term solution I can offer is that the Kenyan government demand a larger stake in some of these mining operations. Mining operations in Kenya could be expanded, thus providing employment for Kenyans and increasing the mining sector of its economy. This, however, would require generous foreign assistance. Cleaning up corruption by providing transparency and accountability for revenues is a crucial factor in determining whether Kenya will receive generous funding for such a project. Considering the state of corruption in Kenya, such ventures may be a long way off.

Agriculture in Kenya

Kenya's market-based economy is largely dependent upon agriculture, yet only half of its subsistence agriculture actually plays a part in the economy. Kenya has been a substantial cultivator of marijuana for many years. Legalization of marijuana would lead to greater state investment, provide much needed employment, and bolster Kenya's overall GDP. If the Kenyan government does not conduct business transactions in a transparent manner, international sanctions could be implemented.

Corruption in Kenya

Unfortunately, sanctions are already informally in place: grand corruption and graft in Kenya have caused the IMF and World Bank to delay loans to the country. According to the ministry of finances in Kenya, the government is losing about $4 billion per year to corrupt officials involved in graft; some of the rewards are as large as 10%.[191]

Continued corruption probes are essential in order to clean up Kenyan politics. Much of this burden falls on Europe, international watchdogs, and of course, the Kenya Anti-Corruption Commission (KACC). The KACC has successfully helped prosecute some of the low level crooks, but higher-ups are still untouched, even though everyone in Kenya knows they are thieves, which implies that there is corruption even within Kenya's High Court—otherwise cases would not be so easily dismissed.

Until corruption is uprooted and the kleptocracy is ended, basic infrastructure will continue to be neglected, and many Kenyans will continue to be deprived of their right to quality healthcare and education. Most troubling of all is that violence between various impoverished ethnic groups may ensue again if government corruption is not resolved.

Liberia

A civil war (1989-2003) left infrastructure in Liberia devastated and caused the UN to impose sanctions on Liberia. Although there have been economic and sociopolitical improvements since the 2005 election of president Ellen

Johnson Sirleaf, and the UN has since dropped its ban on diamonds, among other industries, there are still problems concerning alluvial diamond mining and Liberia's rubber plantations. As with many other African countries, there is widespread poverty and illiteracy. What I find most interesting is that unemployment is also extremely high in Liberia (85%)[192], which I will discuss below.

Labor Rights Issues

Additionally, there are still instances of forced labor and illegal child labor in alluvial diamond mines[193], despite the fact that Liberia joined the Kimberly Process in 2007. Another destination for forced labor trafficking victims is Firestone's rubber plantation, one of the largest rubber plantations in the world. Activists and NGO's have petitioned Firestone to amend working conditions on the plantation, which are literally backbreaking. For instance, the rubber tappers "must carry two heavy buckets of raw latex weighing 75 pounds each on both ends of a stick on their back for miles".[194]

Economic Issues

According to the Heritage Foundation's 2011 Economic Index, Liberia ranked fairly low across the board in Economic Freedom. In particular, lack of financial freedom, lack of property rights and prevalence of corruption are holding the country back. As a result of endemic corruption, foreign investment is still weak in Liberia. As is the case in Democratic Republic of Congo, there is much illegal mining of gold and diamonds, which is costing Liberia's government about $25 million per year.[195]

Solutions

There is light at the end of tunnel, provided that Liberia roots out corruption. There are suspected reserves of offshore oil that can be exploited in the near future, which would increase employment in Liberia.[196] Cultivation of cannabis is on the rise in Liberia. The legalization of marijuana will provide an important source of employment in Liberia's agricultural sector, and contribute to the poor country's overall GDP. As for the rest of the poor indigenous people of Liberia who are currently "unemployed", so long as they are protected from rebel activities spilling over the border from C'ote d'Ivoire, and so long as they are provided with more comprehensive medical care, many of them will continue to regard their impoverishment with ambivalence.

Mali

The government of Mali stabilized after the 1992 ratification of a democratic Constitution, modeled after Western politics. This resulted in the creation of a Democratic Republic and increased political relations with Canada. Canada has been most important in helping Mali's mining industry to grow; moreover, their practices are relatively environmentally sound, which encourages more diplomacy and trust in Western powers. Canada has built trust with Mali by investing in the production of railways, hydroelectric power, and improvement of telecommunications.

Although Canadian companies have improved the lifestyle of many Malian people, it is important to understand that imperfections remain in their companies' mining practices. In particular, the Kidal Region, created by the Malian government for the Tuareg peoples, is subject to some levels of pollution, disease, and poverty. Mining companies should address issues of pollution as this can damage crops that are necessary for creating and maintaining a sustainable society.

Mali is host to many other indigenous peoples, such as the Mande, Bambara, Moor, and the Songhai groups. Many of these groups live in the Gao Region, where much of joint ventures with Canada's mining companies are taking place. At the moment, there is peace and content among these groups, even though they live in abject poverty. My economic revolution will ensure that peace is maintained in Mali.

Niger

After decades of conflicts between the Niger Armed Forces and the Tuareg and Toubou ethnic groups of Niger and Mali, the nation of Niger finds itself in a stable position of peace, yet the economy of the country is suffering due to the Massive 2010 Drought and resulting famine that struck most of the Sahel Belt.

After a peaceful military coup in February 2010, former Niger president Mamadou Tandja was overthrown after rewriting the constitution to extend his reign. Salou Djibo took power as Head of the Military Government, and installed Mahamadou Danda as the Civilian Prime Minister. This resulted in Niger being expelled from the African Union, yet both leaders promise peace with a new movement called The Supreme Council for Restoration of Democracy. Djibo has past connections serving with UN Peacekeeping Forces in Côte d'Ivoire and the Democratic Republic of Congo; Danda served as the Political Counselor at the Canadian Embassy to Niger. A spokesman for the coup said: "We call on national and international opinions to support us in our patriotic action to save Niger and its population from poverty, deception, and corruption".[197]

According to the CIA: "Future growth may be sustained by exploitation of oil, gold, coal, and other mineral resources." I call upon the international community to help this poor, landlocked country by increasing investment in these mineral resources. The African Union should reverse its opinion of the Supreme Council in Niger.

Nigeria

Nigeria, the 8th most populous country on the planet, is characterized by extreme political and social corruption: "Corruption is endemic at all levels of government and society, and the president, vice president, governors, and deputy governors are constitutionally immune from civil and criminal prosecution."[198] Money laundering is an ongoing concern: "Proceeds from drug trafficking, oil theft or bunkering, bribery and embezzlement, contraband smuggling, theft, corruption, and financial crimes, such as bank fraud, real estate fraud, and identity theft, constitute major sources of illicit proceeds in Nigeria."[199] As a result of embezzlement and mismanagement of oil revenues in particular, basic infrastructure has remained underdeveloped and poverty continues to be widespread.[200] Although President Goodluck Jonathan is a positive change for Nigeria, corruption, inefficient governance and human rights violations remain ongoing concerns.

Fraud and embezzlement are significant issues in Nigeria:

> Advance fee fraud, also known as "419" fraud in reference to the fraud section in Nigeria's criminal code, remains a lucrative financial crime that generates hundreds of millions of illicit dollars annually. Money laundering in Nigeria takes many forms, including investment in real estate; wire transfers to offshore banks; political party financing; deposits in foreign bank accounts; use of professional services, such as lawyers, accountants, and investment advisers; and cash smuggling.[201]

Property rights are severely lacking as well:

> Nigeria's judiciary suffers from corruption, delays, insufficient funding, a severe lack of available court facilities, a lack of computerized systems for document processing, and unscheduled adjournments of court sessions because of power outages. One of the world's least efficient property registration systems makes acquiring and maintaining rights to real property difficult. Enforcement of copyrights, patents, and trademarks is weak.[202]

Human Rights

Human rights violations continue to be a crisis in Nigeria: "Intercommunal, political, and sectarian violence has claimed the lives of more than 15,000 people since the end of military rule in 1999."[203] Government corruption and mismanagement of resources only serve to fuel militant and ethnic violence:

> Widespread poverty and poor governance in Nigeria have created an environment where militant groups thrive. A spate of politically motivated killings by Islamist militants in the north, and continued kidnappings and violence by Niger Delta militants—including the brazen Independence Day bombing in Abuja, the capital, for which they claimed responsibility—raised concern about stability in the run-up to planned 2011 general elections.[204]

In 2010, thousands of people died in the Plateau State alone as a result of sectarian and intercommunal violence. In the capital Jos, there is continuing violent confict, such as targeted machete killings "with the mostly Christian Berom group" pitted "against the largely Muslim Hausa and Fulani groups."[205] Murray Last, an anthropologist at University College in London and an expert on Nigeria, said about the sectarian violence in Jos: "It is not about religion."[206] According to Last, "[Religion] is just the glove that covers the hand. That hand is politics: the access to power and the access to land."[207]

The security forces of Nigeria are thoroughly corrupt:

> Again in 2010, members of the Nigeria Police Force were widely implicated in the extortion of money and the arbitrary arrest and torture of criminal suspects and

others. They solicited bribes from victims of crimes to initiate investigations, and from suspects to drop investigations. They were also implicated in numerous extrajudicial killings of persons in custody. Meanwhile senior police officials embezzle and mismanage funds intended for basic police operations. They also enforce a perverse system of "returns," in which rank-and-file officers pay a share of the money extorted from the public up the chain of command.[208]

Endemic corruption is the root cause of Nigeria's violent conflicts. Nigeria's government has not made significant progress in addressing issues of corruption. For instance, Nigeria's National Assembly did not pass the Freedom of Information bill to improve transparency. Moreover, anti-corruption campaigns have not been running smoothly: "Targeted attacks against anti-corruption officials increased significantly in 2010. Gunmen in three separate incidents shot and killed anti-corruption personnel, including the head of the forensic unit and a former senior investigator."[209] Not surprisingly, "Perpetrators of all classes of human rights violations [enjoy] near-total impunity . . . while widespread police abuses and the mismanagement and embezzlement of Nigeria's vast oil wealth [continue] unabated."[210]

Marijuana Cultivation

Nigeria needs to broaden its economic base by creating more service and industry-based jobs, which will be difficult to do until corruption is rooted out. In the meantime, agriculture makes up 70% of Nigeria's labor force, and most of these laborers are poverty-stricken. Since agriculture only accounts for roughly a third of Nigeria's GDP, it would be a benefit to poor agricultural laborers if the production and use of marijuana were legalized. According to the US Dept of State:

> In Nigeria, the only drug cultivated in significant amounts domestically is cannabis sativa (marijuana). Nigerian-grown marijuana is the most common drug abused in the country. It is also exported to neighboring West African countries through Nigeria's vast porous borders and then shipped to Europe.[211]

Clearly, legalization of production and use of marijuana could be quite lucrative for Nigerian entrepreneurs. Overall GDP could be drastically boosted by domestic sales and exports, thus significantly reducing poverty levels.

Conclusion

Government corruption is the single greatest threat to the welfare of the people of Nigeria. Inadequate infrastructure continues to be hindered by corruption: "Domestic and foreign observers recognize corruption as a serious obstacle to economic growth and poverty reduction", which, in conjunction with crime, is a "disincentive" to invest in Nigeria's future.[212] The National Assembly of Nigeria should pass transparency legislation, and provide better protection for anti-corruption personnel. Unfortunately, until corruption and government-sponsored theft are significantly reduced, violence will continue in Nigeria.

Senegal

Senegal is a candidate for minimal development. Nearly half of the country is unemployed. Agriculture accounts for 77.5% of the labor force and 14.9% of the GDP.[213] Legalization of cannabis might help to improve employment and raise overall GDP:

> Cannabis, a traditionally popular drug in Senegal, is cultivated in the south, in the Casamance region. According to UNODC, Senegal may become the leading producer of cannabis among the Francophone countries of West Africa and the third largest producer in West Africa after Nigeria and Ghana.[214]

Sierra Leone

Sierra Leone is very similar to neighboring country Liberia. There is an overall lack of rights and lack of respect for the indigenous people, and corruption is perceived as widespread. From the CIA: "Sierra Leone is an extremely poor nation with tremendous inequality in income distribution. While it possesses substantial mineral, agricultural, and fishery resources, its physical and social infrastructure has yet to recover from the civil war, and serious social disorders continue to hamper economic development."[215]

Formal property rights are virtually non-existent in Sierra Leone. "There is no land titling system, and judicial corruption is significant."[216] Foreign investment in Sierra Leone is also hindered by judicial corruption and slowness. For instance, many in Sierra Leone were outraged by the government's corrupt deal with London Mining Company, which was "shrouded in secrecy", citing that the company was given an unreasonably large ten-year 20% tax break.[217] Many have called for revisions to Sierra Leone's contract with London Mining Company—with this I agree.

Many of Sierra Leone's potential solutions are similar to Liberia's. Sierra Leone's laws need to be revised so as to grant sovereignty to the various indigenous tribes—whose "traditional tribal justice systems continue to serve as a supplement to the central government's judiciary."[218] Also similar to Liberia is the potential for offshore oil drilling and the potential for state-controlled cannabis cultivation, both of which would contribute greatly to the poverty stricken country's GDP. The peaceful democratic elections in 2007 were a hopeful sign that Sierra Leone will continue to develop its economy, improve its judiciary, and ultimately reduce internal corruption to an acceptable level.

South Africa

As a result of its strategic location and abundance of natural resources, South Africa is a "middle-income, emerging market."[219] Despite social changes and economic reform, "poverty is widespread, and much of the population is poorly educated and lacks access to infrastructure and services."[220] Corruption is the major obstacle to improving South Africa's economy:

Official corruption, particularly in the police and the Department of Home Affairs, is viewed as widespread. In 2008, Parliament voted to disband the South African Police Anti-Corruption Unit and the Directorate for Special Operations and fold their jurisdiction into a new high-priority crimes unit, known as the Hawks, under the South African Police Service.[221]

The previous anti-corruption unit, dubbed The Scorpions, was disbanded because too many of its investigators were being killed. In its place, The Hawks have formed a Directorate for Priority Crime Investigation. The new unit "has formed a close working relationship with the Department of Justice and Constitutional Development, the National Treasury, the Financial Intelligence Centre, the South African Revenue Service, and the Department of Home Affairs."[222]

Despite corruption, South Africa's "well-developed financial, legal, communications, energy, and transport sectors"[223] serve as an example for the rest of Africa. Its "stock exchange . . . is the 18th largest in the world; and modern infrastructure [supports] a relatively efficient distribution of goods to major urban centers throughout the region."[224]

Uganda

Like so many other African countries, corruption is the primary factor preventing improvement in human rights, and has, in many cases, only served to exacerbate rural poverty and ethnic violence. Investigations have found that Uganda has neglected to combat corruption at the highest levels—this "bureaucratic apathy contributes to perceptions of corruption."[225] Since 1990, Uganda has received approximately $2 billion in foreign aid and debt relief.[226] Unfortunately, this aid "is misappropriated or . . . outright swindled and the balance officially used by those in leadership".[227] For instance:

> Anti-malarial medicines and bed nets provided by donor nations like China and the U.S. are being sold on the black market in Uganda. And not only are organized crime gangs to blame, but President Yoweri Museveni's own investigation found that a number of government officials, including the three senior Health Ministry officials who manage the national malaria control program, are among those involved in the theft of government drugs. These culprits steal anti-malarial pills and nets, and then sell them to fake clinics, keeping the profits for themselves.[228]

Rebel Threat

The Lord's Resistance Army (LRA) was formed in 1987 as an opposition to Uganda's corrupt government. Its ideology is based upon Christianity and Mysticism, a powerful combination that has contributed to its longevity. The LRA is responsible for the murder of thousands of innocent civilians, mass rape, and the displacement of 2 million people in Uganda since the 1990's.[229] Recently, their range of activity has increased; the group has gained a foothold in the Democratic Republic of Congo, Chad, Sudan, and Central African Republic. In 2009, according to the UN, "in a 10-month rampage of killings, rape and mutilation in neighbouring countries . . . the LRA killed some 1,300 civilians, abducted 1,400 more, including hundreds of children and women, and displaced nearly 300,000 others."[230] In 2009 and 2010, the LRA expanded it ranks with mass recruitment, and according to Human Rights Watch, "the group had brutally abducted at least 697 adults and children."[231]

Although evidence is difficult to come by, my guess is that the rebels are attempting to overtake resources such as gold mines, similar to the operations of the Hutu Power FDLR in the Congo. Just as government corruption contributes to the continued presence of the FDLR in Congo, so too has it fueled the LRA's ongoing struggle in Uganda and neighboring countries. To this end, these rebel groups are violently revolting against harsh poverty caused by government neglect and outright corruption. Their contempt for the government is surpassed only by their contempt for other ethnic groups, whom they perceive as inferior.

A 2009 article in *The Guardian* succinctly sums up the problem: "Corruption has become so endemic in Uganda; it is an accepted way of life".[232] This is unacceptable. The corrupt politicians need to be removed as soon as possible.

Zimbabwe

There is much uncertainty and debate about the economic future of Zimbabwe, one of the poorest countries in Africa, but one thing is certain: the Zimbabwe African National Union-Patriotic Front (ZANU-PF) and its leader,

President Robert Mugabe, provide a clear-cut example of the failure of far left authoritarianism to uphold human rights. The various crises include:

1. Widespread Famine, affecting 20-34% of the population.
2. An HIV epidemic affecting 14.3% (1.2 million) of the population.
3. Unemployment level at 95%.
4. Poverty level at 68%.
5. Violations of human rights, discussed below.

The CIA's take is that, despite human rights crises, severe budget deficit, * and many years of hyperinflation, Zimbabwe's economy is improving: "The power-sharing government formed in February 2009 has led to some economic improvements, including the cessation of hyperinflation by eliminating the use of the Zimbabwe dollar and removing price controls."[233] Moreover, Zimbabwe's economy posted real growth of 5.9% in 2010.[234] The Heritage Foundation, on the other hand, believes that extreme government interventions, land reforms and years of hyperinflation are causing Zimbabwe's economy to fail: "In recent years, the financial sector has contracted significantly amid continuing uncertainty over economic policies and macroeconomic instability caused by the government."[235] In particular, the agriculture sector "has been crippled by expropriation of white-owned commercial farms."[236]

Landlaw Corruption

As one might expect, government corruption is a severe problem: "Commercial banks, building societies, moneylenders, insurance brokers, realtors, and lawyers in Zimbabwe are all vulnerable to exploitation by money launderers."[237] Fraud is endemic in property seizures: "Top officials hand-pick multiple farms and register them in the names of family members to evade the official one-farm policy, and individuals aligned with top officials are allowed to seize land that is not designated for acquisition."[238]

Expropriations of private property are already out of hand in Zimbabwe, yet, despite EU sanctions, Mugabe remains obstinate in continuing down the path of corruption. He threatened to step up government enforcement of expropriations as a retaliation to international sanctions: "We can read the riot act and say this is 51 percent we are taking and if the sanctions persist we are taking over 100 percent."[239] Already, more than 700,000 people have lost their homes, and/or their jobs as a result of the 2005 Operation Murambatsvina.[240]

The operation is a part of Mugabe's indigenization plan, which is essentially about promoting black empowerment, whereby farmland owned by entrepreneurs (white people) is confiscated and given to indigenous black people. According to the Heritage Foundation: "The government has expropriated land without compensating investors."[241] The Southern African Development Community (SAPC), an inter-governmental organization affiliated with the African Union, and its tribunal opposed Mugabe by ruling in favor of 79 white farmers in 2008.[242] Mugabe refused to enforce these rulings by the tribunal and formally withdrew Zimbabwe from the SAPC. Clearly, Mugabe's land reform is too extreme both in its method and in its swiftness.

Diamond Corruption

The diamond mining industry is rife with corruption in Zimbabwe. Young men and children are illegally forced by Zimbabwean "government security forces" and soldiers to work in the diamond fields of Marange district.[243] Forced laborers are subjected to beatings and harassment, yet Zimbabwe's government has "failed to investigate or prosecute."[244] Soldiers smuggle out diamonds[245] and execute other illegal miners—these government-sanctioned murders have drawn much international criticism. Both the CIA and Human Rights Watch have indicated, money laundering "may also be magnified by opportunities to smuggle diamonds". According to Human Rights Watch:

> Diamond revenue, particularly from the Marange diamond fields in eastern Zimbabwe, is providing a parallel source of revenue for ZANU-PF and its repressive state apparatus. Companies with connections to ZANU-PF are mining diamonds in Marange, where military control and abuses continue. The diamond revenues continue to benefit a few senior people in the government and their associates rather than the people of Zimbabwe.[246]

---

1   *   The CIA also lists "Zimbabwe's 1998-2002 involvement in the war in the Democratic Republic of the Congo" as a significant detriment to Zimbabwe, citing that it "drained hundreds of millions of dollars" from its fragile economy.

Despite continued diamond smuggling and illegal forced labor in the Marange diamond fields, both South Africa and the Kimberly Process allow Zimbabwe to "legally" export diamonds. Part of the problem is that its "mandate narrowly defines 'blood diamonds' as those mined by abusive rebel groups, not abusive governments."[247]

Political Violence and Human Rights Violations

Mugabe's oppressive ZANU-PF is the greatest threat to political reform in Zimbabwe. Similar to corrupt authoritarian governments of communist nations, Mugabe and political elites place the success of the nation, and more importantly, their own personal wealth before the welfare of the people. Mugabe's duplicity is also very similar to the leaders of communist nations in that he pretends to give a damn about Zimbabweans by consistently playing a phony race card while also allowing grave human rights violations to go unnoticed. According to Human Rights Watch:

> Two years into Zimbabwe's power-sharing government, President Robert Mugabe and the Zimbabwe African National Union-Patriotic Front (ZANU-PF), have used violence and repression to continue to dominate government institutions and hamper meaningful human rights progress. The power-sharing government has not investigated widespread abuses, including killings, torture, beatings, and other ill-treatment committed by the army, ZANU-PF supporters, and officials against real and perceived supporters of the MDC.

> The former opposition party, the Movement
> for Democratic Change (MDC), lacks real
> power to institute its political agenda and
> end human rights abuses.[248]

Conclusion

Mugabe and ZANU-PF are totalitarian in nature,
which compromises the entire government of Zimbabwe.
The problem is that the corrupt executive branch "strongly
influences the judiciary and openly challenges court
outcomes"[249]. This places the political and business elites of
Zimbabwe "above the law". In response, the EU has placed
sanctions on Zimbabwe that have included the freezing
of assets of corrupt individuals and businesses, and arms
embargos. In February 2011, the EU removed 35 people
from its list of visa bans, however, it ruled to keep 163
officials and business partners, and 31 businesses on its list
of sanctions for another year.[250]

These sanctions are very fair, as they target the crooked
politicians, however, when one considers that the EU and
the US have also scaled back on provisions of food aid
on humanitarian grounds[251], this could be considered an
unofficial "sanction" on Zimbabwe. Even though Mugabe
is correct in stating that his people are being "punished" by
international sanctions, it is ultimately Mugabe's corruption
and stubborn retaliations that are responsible for much
of the problems facing the poverty-stricken populace of
Zimbabwe. Mugabe and Zimbabwe's government must
be held responsible for creating a sustainable economy
in Zimababwe, not the EU. In this light, his criticisms of
international policy are irrelevant and only serve to distract

from rampant internal corruption and human rights abuses, both of which hinder Zimbabwe's development as a nation.

Solution for Change

The totalitarianism of ZANU-PF is beginning to resemble the one-party politics of nations like North Korea and China. The Movement for Democratic Change (MDC) has been the strongest opposition party to ZANU-PF. The MDC is the ideal political party to create progressive reform in Zimbabwe. If the people of Zimbabwe want their freedom, they must advocate for peaceful change using the political ideology of the MDC.

Conclusion

Some countries did not get a mention because they face similar issues to the countries I've already discussed. They will depend on the international aid, the African Union and their neighbors for continued economic development. Many of these countries are candidates for minimal development. Other countries are embroiled in civil wars or they are caught in the vice-like grip of totalitarian dictators. Guinea is struggling to reform its economy after a military coup was overthrown and replaced by a transitional government. Rwanda suffers from incessant political instability and impenetrable corruption. Mozambique needs to reform its banking system—government subsidies make it a particularly good target for peaceful revolution. Ghana needs to industrialize further in order to improve infrastructure. Tanzania's court system is in need of extensive revisions. The list of problems goes on and on, but the primary problem is that economic improvements are set back by endemic government corruption.

To conclude on a positive note, the battle for economic freedom in Africa is being fought by JFPI Corporation, Africa's largest holding company. The corporate conglomerate represents all 53 nations of Africa and champions Black Economic Empowerment. JFPI Corporation will probably become increasingly important in continued development of Africa's market-based economy.

CHAPTER 4

The Greater Middle East

The Greater Middle East is characterized by a high concentration of Arab people, most of whom live in poverty. As a result widespread poverty, thousands of people have taken to the streets in various North African and Middle Eastern countries:

> The catalysts for the revolts in all Northern African and Gulf countries have been the concentration of wealth in the hands of autocrats in power for decades, insufficient transparency of its redistribution, corruption, and especially the refusal of the youth to accept the status quo. Increasing food prices and global famine rates have also been a significant factor, as they involve threats to food security worldwide and prices that approach levels of the 2007-2008 world food price crisis. In countries like Armenia, high rates of inflation have been cited as a cause for unrest.[252]

As a result of clashes between protestors and security forces, as well as self-immolations, thousands of people have died in these protests. Fortunately, my socioeconomic theory could bring an end to all of these protests, thus restoring some political stability to North Africa and the Middle East.

Afghanistan

From the CIA: "Afghanistan's economy is recovering from decades of conflict. The economy has improved significantly since the fall of the Taliban regime in 2001 largely because of the infusion of international assistance, the recovery of the agricultural sector, and service sector growth."[253] Nevertheless, it will take decades to make significant improvements in Afghanistan's economy because it is landlocked and resource poor. As many farmers rely on sales and distribution of poppy straw, cultivation of these poppies should be completely unrestricted.

Algeria

Algeria is slated for maximum human development. Crucial economic issues the Algerian government needs to address include:

1. Increasing limited foreign ownership.
2. Improving access to foreign exchange.
3. Banking reform, including an increase in privately owned assets.
4. Revising property rights legislation so that it is easier to understand.

5. Improving the efficiency of the judiciary and providing consistency in rulings.[254]

Fortunately, inflation in food prices will no longer be an issue if my socioeconomic theory is implemented. This, in and of itself, will increase political stability in Algeria so that it may pursue economic reforms.

Armenia

Armenia is characterized by corruption, extreme poverty, and low unemployment:

> Corruption is perceived as widespread and even pervasive. Demands for bribes by government officials are routine. Government-connected businesses hold monopolies on the importation of numerous vital products. The judicial system is still recovering from underdevelopment and corruption—legacies of the Soviet era that substantially impede the enforcement of contracts.[255]

Reducing corruption in Armenia must necessarily precede economic reform. As with Algeria, inflation in food prices will no longer be a concern if my socioeconomic theory is accepted.

Azerbaijan

According to the Heritage Foundation:

> Azerbaijan's judicial system, filled with bureaucratic requirements and generally seen as corrupt and inefficient, does not function independently of the executive. The poor quality, reliability, and transparency of governance, as well as regulatory abuse and poor contract enforcement, significantly impede the ability of many companies to do business. Corruption is perceived as rampant. Azerbaijan ranks 143rd out of 180 countries in Transparency International's Corruption Perceptions Index for 2009. Judicial and police corruption is widespread. Arbitrary tax and customs administration creates opportunities for graft, regulatory practices favor monopolies, and corruption exists at all levels. Politically connected businesses have achieved control of several lucrative sectors of the economy.[256]

Corruption is a continuing obstacle to economic freedom in Azerbaijan. It is entirely unpredictable as to what the future holds for Azerbaijan.

Egypt

Egypt is ready for the reform of the food economy: "the government still heavily subsidizes food, energy, and other key commodities".[257] However, "enforcement of intellectual property rights is seriously deficient" and "bribery of low-level civil servants seems to be a part of daily life".[258] As of this writing, Egypt is in the middle of a civil war. Hopefully they can resolve this peacefully with the help of my socioeconomic theory.

Georgia

High unemployment, corruption, and judicial deficiencies plague Georgia, however, improvements are being made:

> Judges now have to pass tests before appointment, but foreigners and Georgians continue to doubt the judicial system's ability to protect private property and contracts. The government has improved its performance in fighting corruption; it has fired thousands of civil servants and police, and several high-level officials have been prosecuted for corruption-related offenses. The law provides criminal penalties for official corruption. While the government implemented these laws effectively against low-level corruption, some non-governmental organizations alleged that senior-level officials engaged in corruption with impunity.[259]

It is encouraging that Georgia is improving its judiciary and addressing institutionalized corruption.

Iran

Iran, the center of the Greater Middle-East, relies heavily on the oil sector. There is important legislation on the table:

> The legislature in late 2009 passed President Mahmud Ahmadi-Nejad's bill to reduce subsidies, particularly on food and energy. The bill would phase out subsidies—which benefit Iran's upper and middle classes the most—over three to five years and replace them with cash payments to Iran's lower classes. However, the start of the program was delayed repeatedly throughout 2010 over fears of public reaction to higher prices.[260]

After the peaceful revolution, Ahmadi-nejad's bill will be able to go through and will be accepted by Iranians because higher food prices will no longer matter.

Iraq

In the midst of an ongoing insurgency, Iraq has made steady economic growth. Oil still continues to be the country's primary source of revenue, and the US continues to be its largest importer. Iraq needs to plan for post peak-oil economics by investing in new resources in order to expand the country's market-based economy beyond oil and textiles. Poverty is still an issue, and, according to the CIA:

> Iraqi leaders remain hard pressed to translate macroeconomic gains into improved lives for ordinary Iraqis. Unemployment remains a problem throughout the country. Reducing corruption and implementing reforms, such as bank restructuring and developing the private sector, would be important steps in this direction.[261]

Forced labor is an ongoing concern: "Iraq is a destination country for men and women who migrate from Bangladesh, India, Indonesia, Nepal, Philippines, Sri Lanka, Thailand, Pakistan, Georgia, Jordan, and Uganda and are subsequently subjected to conditions of forced labor as construction workers, security guards, cleaners, handymen, and domestic workers."[262]

Conclusion

Once my economic revolution is accepted in Iraq, poverty will be reduced and Iraqi leaders can focus on building crucial infrastructure.

Jordan

Jordan faces many obstacles:

> Jordan's economy is among the smallest in the Middle East, with insufficient supplies of water, oil, and other natural resources, underlying the government's heavy reliance on foreign assistance. Other economic challenges for the government

include chronic high rates of poverty, unemployment, inflation, and a large budget deficit.[263]

Corruption may need to be addressed:

Influence peddling and a lack of transparency have been alleged in government procurement and dispute settlement. The use of family, business, and other personal connections to advance personal business interests is seen by many Jordanians as a normal part of doing business.[264]

This country will benefit greatly from my theory.

Kazakhstan

Huge oil reserves and macroeconomic reforms have helped Kazakhstan to become a middle-income country; it is the paragon of human development in Central Asia. Kazakhstan needs to improve foreign investment:

Screening of foreign investment proposals is often non-transparent, arbitrary, and slow, and foreign ownership in some sectors is limited. An unclear legal code, legislative favoritism toward Kazakh companies, inconsistent application of regulations, and government interference in commercial operations further deter investment. Only domestic citizens and companies may own land.[265]

Amendments to Kazakh law, more consistent enforcement of regulations and less emphasis on nationalism will only serve to improve Kazakhstan's foreign investment climate.

Kyrgyzstan

Ongoing concerns in Kyrgyzstan include: "endemic corruption, poor interethnic relations",[266] as well as "external debt, heavy dependence on foreign aid, a thriving black market, a high crime rate, Islamist radicalism, and drug smuggling."[267] Clearly, this country is a charity case, and must struggle to overcome its various obstacles to economic development and freedom.

Lebanon

Lebanon faces one crucial issue: Ottoman law[268] needs to be updated so its judiciary can function more efficiently.

Libya

Libya is supported by substantial oil reserves, which "provide about 95 percent of Libya's export revenues and well over half of its GDP."[269] Libya's oil wealth allows the country to import 75% of is food needs, however, 1/3 of the population still lives in poverty. Libya's economic freedom is hindered by too much government regulation. In short, Libya's government should:

1. Reduce government business restrictions and bureaucratic interference.
2. Cap government spending.

3. Make concessions for a slight increase in private control of assets.
4. Improve flexibility in labor rights.

My socioeconomic theory would significantly bolster Libya's economy if it were put to use since it would not spend as much of its budget on food.

Morocco

Morocco's economy has made steady improvements despite the global economic crisis. Morocco is currently experiencing political unrest, despite human rights improvements:

> Morocco enjoys a moderately free press, but the government occasionally takes action against journalists who report on three broad subjects considered to be taboo: the monarchy, Islam, and the status of Western Sahara. Influenced by protests elsewhere in the Middle East and North Africa, thousands of Moroccans in February 2011 rallied in Rabat and several other major cities to demand constitutional reform and more democracy and to protest government corruption and high food prices.[270]

As a result of the food revolution, high food prices will become irrelevant, protesting will be quelled, and peace will return to King Mohammed VI's kingdom.

Pakistan

Pakistan is classified as an Islamic Federal Republic, but this name is a bit misleading—the Pakistan People's Party (PPP), a center-left social democratic party, has exclusively controlled the country since 1967. The nepotism of the PPP resembles a regime—the Bhutto family and the Zardari family have uncontested control of the party. Many Pakistanis protest the perceived corruption and authoritarianism of the PPP, and in particular, its current president, Asif Ali Zardari (Mr. 10%), who has been jailed for past corruption charges including the acceptance of multinational bribe money. As a result of corruption and mismanagement, the poverty level is at 24%; healthcare, education and electricity remain under-funded.[271]

Corruption in Pakistan

According to a 2008 Transparency International report, there is rampant institutionalized political corruption. Kickbacks represent 25% of the budget in public service sectors, which has hampered equitable distribution of power, utilities, and other basic infrastructure.[272] This is partially guesswork, since information on government expenditures is not made public.[273] There are past examples however, such as the 1996 SGS scandal involving president Zardari and his deceased wife, former prime minister Benazir Bhutto, in which the two accepted about $15 million worth of bribe money. In regards to kickbacks, the corruption of the government under the PPP is very similar to the corruption of Venezuela, another socialist democracy.

Pakistan is a major recipient of aid from international donor agencies—corruption in government handling of this capital "has adversely affected poverty, aid and development projects."[274] As a result of corruption and negligence, many World Bank programs such as the Baluchistan Primary Education Project have been suspended or cancelled—this has been confirmed both by the Auditor General of Pakistan and the World Bank Country Assistance Foundation.[275] Additionally, the National Anti-Corruption Bureau (NAB), "asserts that 200 billion rupees of financial resources are being wasted through corrupt practices at higher government levels, while 67 billion rupees have fallen prey to lower level corruption every year." However, due to corruption within the Auditor General's office, and, unfortunately, within NAB itself, prosecutions are politically motivated, and have not effectively cracked down on internal corruption in Pakistan.[276] Corruption is also prevalent "in the police, land administration institutions, the judiciary, education, and local governments regarded as the most corrupt public-sector institutions."[277]

Forced Labor in Pakistan

As in India, bonded labor is a human rights issue of grave proportions in Pakistan. Bonded labor revolves primarily around agriculture, brick-making, and "to a lesser extent mining and carpet-making".[278] These activities are "concentrated in the Sindh and Punjab provinces".[279] The US Department of State estimates that the number of "bonded labor victims, including men, women, and children, vary widely, but are likely well over one million."[280]

Conclusion

Corruption is the primary obstacle to economic freedom in Pakistan. Property rights are rudimentary, and hampered by a weak judiciary. Currently Pakistan's government is a combination of English civil law and Islamic law. Nevertheless, the socioeconomic revolution will be a success in Pakistan.

Somalia

Somalia is in the midst of a civil war and represents an extreme humanitarian crisis. Information on Somalia's economy is very difficult to come by—there are few details available. From the US Department of State's Report on narcotics:

> Somalia is the world's quintessential failed state. A fragile transitional federal government controls only portions of the country's capital and remote pockets of some regions. That government is besieged by a classic insurgency, led by U.S.-designated foreign terrorist organization, al-Shabaab. Many ministries exist in name only, or have non-functioning, mostly unpaid staff. There is no court system to speak of, and policing is rudimentary. Any laws that do exist are currently unenforceable given the security threat to the government and its lack of capacity. The financial system in Somalia operates almost completely outside government oversight on the black

> market, or via international money transfer
> companies known as hawalas.[281]

Somali Pirates

Somali Pirates board foreign ships, and, using various weapons such as RPG-7s (rocket-propelled grenade launchers), AKMs (Kalishnikovs) and AK47s, collect ransom money in exchange for the release of the crew and cargo. There is an interesting little back-story to how all this got started. Illegal fishing and toxic dumping in Somali waters became an international "free-for-all" after the start of the Somali Civil War in 1991. Although it is not well publicized, Somali piracy arose as a way to compensate for revenues lost on poached fish and as a means to discourage European and Asian companies from dumping their toxic waste in Somali waters.[282] European and Asian trawlers poach approximately $300 million worth of fish per year from Somali waters.[283]

Piracy has led to some minor improvements business improvements in Somalia's coastal towns, but, by and large, it is a detriment to Somalia, and a hindrance to the many countries whose ships must pass through the Suez Canal. Somali piracy has cost the international community between $7-$12 billion due to increased shipping fees.[284] Egypt has lost about $642 million as a result of Somali piracy since fewer ships have used the Suez canal lately.[285] Additionally, piracy is an impediment to the delivery of food aid shipments. Some countries, such as England, have responded to piracy by sending warships into Somali waters, but this has not had any appreciable affect, since the pirates' ransom income has since increased from $58 million in 2009 to $238 million in 2010.[286]

Crises

1.1 million of Somalia's poverty-stricken population is displaced as a result of the ongoing war.[287] According to the Food and Agriculture Organization of the United Nations, in 2008, 35% of Somali's were undernourished.[288] Although data is not reliable for 2011, malnourishment remains a crisis in Somalia, however, "due to armed attacks on and threats to humanitarian aid workers, the World Food Programme partially suspended its operations in southern Somalia in early January 2010 pending improvement in the security situation."[289]

Conclusion

International NGO's should step up criticism of fish poaching in Somalia's waters; this might end Somali piracy. Clearly, the only sustainable solution to the problem is to ask European and Asian countries to stop illegal dumping and poaching. As for the war, it is uncertain what the outcome will be.

Sudan

Sudan still remains one of the least developed countries in the world.[290] The poverty rate is an alarming 40%.[291] Sudan currently ranks 1.6 on Transparency International's Corruption Index,[292] meaning it is one of the most corrupt countries in the world. Two simultaneous wars—the Darfur War and Sudan's Second Civil War—were officially ended by a Comprehensive Peace Agreement, which was signed in 2005.

The Secession of the South

One of the key agreements of the Comprehensive Peace Agreement in 2005 was to hold a referendum in order to determine if Southern Sudan, an autonomous region, would secede from the North. The referendum was finally held in January 2011—there was an overwhelming majority vote to secede from the North. The new state, called the Republic of South Sudan, launched in July 2011.

Nearly a third of Sudan's economy is based upon petroleum exports, 85% of which are located in the Southern Sudan. China National Petroleum Corporation has a 40% stake in Southern Sudan's oil industry, with significant remaining portions belonging to Malaysia and India. Since 2005, North and South Sudan have been splitting oil profits 50-50.[293] Although a new oil deal is being worked out, oil revenues have still not had an appreciable effect on Sudan's poor infrastructure. Sudapet only has a 5% share—this should be increased in order to provide Sudan more employment in the oil industry and to improve infrastructure with oil revenues.

Chinese and Russia Investments

China is the largest investor in the Sudan, purchasing more than 60% of Sudan's oil exports. Sudan also recently entered into a 9-year agreement to allow Chinese companies to develop its ports on the Red Sea[294] and has recently agreed to invest in Sudanese solar energy.[295] This is just the tip of the iceberg—there are many other Sino-Sudanese investments being planned. Not surprisingly, Bashir recently asked Russia to invest in Northern Sudanese energy not long after striking a deal with China.[296] Furthermore, Russia is currently in talks to begin mining in Northern Sudan for tungsten, a mineral that is used in the production of armaments.[297]

Conclusion

Chinese and Russian investments are important to improving Sudan's infrastructure. Although President Bashir's human rights track record has been abysmal, the deals he has brokered with China and Russia will ultimately improve human development in Sudan.

Syria

Syria is a lower middle-income country, whose wealth is based upon oil. Syria may need a complete overhaul in its corrupt legal system:

> Arbitrary and non-transparent changes in investment law, burdensome bureaucracy, political instability, corruption, and the lack of an independent judiciary undermine investment in Syria's economy. Corruption cuts across most sectors of society and affects the legal system as well. Under-the-table payments are commonplace, as corruption is endemic in nearly all levels of government.[298]

Corruption and heavy government regulation only serve to hold Syria back. It seems that Syria is not on the path to economic reform.

Tajikistan

Under the authoritarian rule of Imomali Rahmon, Tajikistan experiences very little economic freedom. Unfortunately, lack of freedom under the conflicting ideologies of the Islamic-democratic coalition and Rahmon's post-communism are only exacerbated by the fact that Rahmon has control of all three branches of government.[299] There is little that can be done to improve this situation at the moment.

Tunisia

Although government economic controls have decreased in the past decade, the people of Tunisia are clamoring for change:

> Street protests that began in Tunis in December 2010 over high unemployment, corruption, widespread poverty, and high food prices escalated in January 2011, culminating in rioting that led to hundreds of deaths.[300]

The socioeconomic food revolution represents positive change for the people of Tunisia. Rioting will cease, and stability will return to the region. Nevertheless, Tunisian government will still need to address several issues, including "privatizing industry, liberalizing the investment code to increase foreign investment, improving government efficiency, reducing the trade deficit, and reducing socioeconomic disparities in the impoverished south and west."[301] My socioeconomic revolution will help with the lattermost problem as well.

Turkey

The Republic of Turkey is struggling with corruption, bribery, and high levels of unemployment and poverty. Nevertheless, the country is still fairly successful.

Turkmenistan

Turkmenistan is characterized by extremely high unemployment and poverty as a result of neglect under an authoritarian Presidential Republic.[302] From the CIA:

> With an authoritarian ex-Communist regime in power and a tribally based social structure, Turkmenistan has taken a cautious approach to economic reform, hoping to use gas and cotton export revenues to sustain its inefficient economy. Privatization goals remain limited. Overall prospects in the near future are discouraging because of widespread internal poverty, endemic corruption, a poor educational system, government misuse of oil and gas revenues, and Ashgabat's reluctance to adopt market-oriented reforms.[303]

Government regulation is hampering economic progress:

> The explosion of the natural gas pipeline linking Turkmenistan to Russia in

2009 highlights the need to broaden Turkmenistan's productive base. The government restricts foreign investment to a few handpicked partners, while the state-controlled financial system limits credit access to political favorites. Burdensome and opaque regulatory systems, the nearly complete absence of property rights, pervasive corruption, and rigid labor regulations further limit private-sector activity.[304]

Additionally, it is quite difficult to "establish and conduct a business" in Turkmenistan, due to outdated regulatory codes and non-transparency.[305] Corruption inhibits economic freedom:

The anti-corruption laws are ineffective. The non-transparency of the economic system and the existence of patronage networks fuel corruption, especially in government procurement and performance requirements. There is a lack of accountability mechanisms as well as fear of government reprisal.[306]

Conclusion

Turkmenistan should move further right on the political compass by deregulating some of its businesses if it wishes to become a more market-oriented economy. This would also help to improve living conditions for its citizens.

Uzbekistan

The humanitarian situation in Uzbekistan could slowly be devolving into a crisis. From the CIA: "Current concerns include terrorism by Islamic militants, economic stagnation, and the curtailment of . . . democratization."[307] The majority Muslim nation suffers under an "authoritarian presidential rule"[308], which undermines improvements in basic human development. Malnourishment affects 10-19% of the population[309] and over a quarter of the population lives below the poverty line. Moreover, "Uzbekistan's human rights record remains abysmal, with no substantive improvement in 2010."[310] Most of these problems can be attributed to corruption and lack of economic freedom. According to the Heritage Foundation:

> Uzbekistan continues to score poorly in most areas of economic freedom. The lack of meaningful progress on reform and the continuing reliance on the energy sector as a source of economic expansion have effectively precluded broader-based economic development. Weak protection of property rights and widespread corruption are significant drags on Uzbekistan's economic freedom, and the poor investment regime lacks transparency and consistent implementation, discouraging business creation or expansion. Foreign-owned businesses view corruption as one of the largest obstacles to foreign direct investment. The law does not forbid government

officials from acting as 'consultants,' a
common method of extracting bribes.[311]

Conclusion

Corruption is the greatest obstacle to economic
freedom in Uzbekistan. That being said, the government of
Uzbekistan needs to expand its service-based economy in
order to improve its GDP, expand its export base in order to
attract more export partners, and clamp down on corruption
in order to attract foreign investment. Greater protection of
property rights is a must if Uzbekistan seeks to become an
upper-middle class country. People will stop protesting if
their needs are fairly met by the government, and this will,
in turn, help to lower instances of human rights violations.

Peace in the Greater Middle East

To conclude, corruption is significant in the Greater
Middle East. Nations of the Greater Middle East, such as
Kazakhstan, need to clamp down on pirating and better
protect intellectual property rights so that money can
be almost endlessly generated by unlimited demand.
Reform of food and consumables in accordance with my
socioeconomic theory would help the business leaders of
the Middle East to consolidate their monetary power and
feed the hungry for free. My hope is that my socioeconomic
theory will thus bring peace to the Middle East through
economic reform. Political leaders will regain the trust of
their kingdoms, however, it will take decades, or perhaps
even longer, to fully address the issue of endemic poverty in
the Greater Middle East.

CHAPTER 5

Europe

Most of Europe represents the pinnacle of economic freedom. In particular, Sweden is a role model for every developed nation of the world—it is one of the top ten developed nations of the world and the fourth least corrupt as well. Norway is the most developed nation in the world. Nevertheless, there is substantial corruption in Europe and many countries are still struggling with macroeconomic reforms and widespread poverty as a result of the collapse of the Soviet Union.

Bosnia & Herzegovina

Ethnic warfare in 1992 drastically altered Bosnia & Herzegovinia's economy. The country is still stabilizing politically:

> The 1995 Dayton Agreement ended three years of war and finalized Bosnia and Herzegovina's secession from the former Yugoslavia. Under a loose central government, two separate entities exist along ethnic lines: the Republika Srpska

(Serbian) and the Federation of Bosnia and Herzegovina (Muslim/Croat). The European Union signed a Stabilization and Association Agreement with Bosnia and Herzegovina in June 2008, moving the country closer to EU membership.[312]

Hopefully Bosnia & Herzegovina succeed in joining the EU as this will help the country to make informed decisions regarding its economic reforms.

Greece

Greece was hit hard by the global economic crisis, and its economy went into recession in 2009. The country's economy is in crisis mode—real growth in GDP decreased by 4.8% in 2010, and unemployment remains high.

Under intense pressure by the EU and international market participants, the government has adopted a medium-term austerity program that includes cutting government spending, reducing the size of the public sector, decreasing tax evasion, reforming the health care and pension systems, and improving competitiveness through structural reforms to the labor and product markets. An uptick in widespread unrest, however, could challenge the government's ability to implement reforms and meet budget targets, and could also lead to rioting or violence.[313]

Fortunately, my socio-economic theory could have a direct positive influence on Greece since its government spending is so high. As a result of adopting the new food economy, the austerity program may be dropped altogether, and peace will be restored to Greece. Nevertheless, Greece will need to continue reforming its economy.

Moldova

Former Soviet-controlled Moldova is plagued by corruption and lack of resources:

> Moldova remains one of the poorest countries in Europe despite recent progress from its small economic base. It enjoys a favorable climate and good farmland but has no major mineral deposits. As a result, the economy depends heavily on agriculture, featuring fruits, vegetables, wine, and tobacco. Moldova must import almost all of its energy supplies.[314]

Moldova's economy will be improved indirectly by my socio-economic revolution, regardless of its food-based economy. The digital revolution would generate billions of dollars for Moldova's various businesses, thus improving overall GDP and increasing human development.

Poland

The invasion by Germany during WWII and the consequent occupation by Soviet Russia have had lasting effects on Poland's infrastructure and economy. After gaining independence from Russia:

> A "shock therapy" program . . . enabled the country to transform its economy into one of the most robust in Central Europe, but Poland still faces the lingering challenges of high unemployment, underdeveloped and dilapidated infrastructure, and a poor rural underclass.[315]

Poland will finally be able to repair its damaged infrastructure after it joins the socioeconomic revolution.

Romania

Romania, a middle-income country, is struggling with translating economic gains into improvement for its impoverished:

> The country emerged in 2000 from a punishing three-year recession thanks to strong demand in EU export markets. Domestic consumption and investment have fueled strong GDP growth in recent years, but have led to large current account imbalances. Romania's macroeconomic gains have only recently started to spur creation of a middle class and address Romania's widespread poverty.[316]

Romania is a prime example of what must economically be accomplished in many African countries. Strong investment in infrastructure and increased domestic consumption will create a strong middle class.

Russia

Post-Yeltsin Russia is characterized by a shrinking workforce, weak property rights, and, above all else, a high level of political corruption.[317] It is rather predictable that Putin's oligarchy would capitalize on the privatization schemes that were born as a result of Yeltsin's market-oriented reforms, thus transforming Russia into a "super-corporation". If Russia wishes to remain a superpower, there can be no other alternative.

Shortly after being elected to the position of President, Putin commented, "A group of FSB colleagues dispatched to work undercover in the government has successfully completed its first mission."[318] Presumably, Putin was referring to substantial gains in personal capital, since personal wealth plays an important part in Post-Yeltsin politics, otherwise known as Putinism.

Although Putinism was a term used to describe the government of The Russian Federation under Putin's control, elements of Putinism have become endemic in Russian politics. One of the crucial paradigms solidified by Putinism was the control of Russia's economy by chekists, the political ruling class of Russia, and the siloviki, politicians handpicked from the security services such as the FSB (Federal Security Service of the Russian Federation). As much as 78% of Russia's top politicians (Siloviks) are ex-KGB or current FSB employees.[319]

Many critics of Russia's government compare Putin's cronyism to organized crime. In particular, there have been accusations of targeted killings, although few details have surfaced. Also, the siloviki in "acting reserve" receive special benefits, such as a 2nd salary, and follow instructions from FSB—they are above the law.[320] The most important aspect of this political system is that much of its operations are conducted with discretion and secrecy, since it is almost exclusively run by the FSB. Putinism lives on despite Dmitry Medvedev's appointment as president of Russia.

Human Rights Violations in Russia

Of particular interest to me was the participation of Russia in North Korea's labor camps. According to the US Dept of State, there are approximately 40,000 prisoners detained in North Korean logging camps operating in the Russian Far East.[321] Although North Korean prisoners are detained in these camps, and the DPRK takes about 35 percent of the camp's profits, the joint-venture is primarily operated by Russian Timber Group.[322]

As one might expect, conditions at these camps are inhumane; prisoners work 12-hour days, with only two "free" days per year; many are executed if they attempt escape.[323] The DPRK withholds as much as 85 percent of the prisoners' wages.[324] Many of the camps' detainees were imprisoned by the DPRK as enemies of North Korea, a trait common to many of the DPRK operated prison camps, which I discussed earlier in the section on North Korea. Although Russian Timber Group is a privately owned company, Russia's government is complicit with North Korea's by allowing the logging camps to operate legally, thereby extending the DPRK's jurisdiction onto Russian soil. Russia should address this human rights violation by asking Russian Timber Group to cease all illegal operations with the DPRK.

Conclusion

Russia is the best example of Western bias concerning economic freedom. Russia scored 50.5 of a possible 100 points for economic freedom on The Heritage Foundation's 2011 Index of Economic Freedom. The Heritage Foundation has consistently deducted points from Russia's scores in economic freedom in the past decade because its government heavily regulates business and neglects the private sector—specifically small businesses. On this basis alone, its economy is considered "less free". The critical point to understand is that Heritage Foundation gauges the "economic freedom" of Russia's elite class in many of its categories. However, the criticism that Russia's economy is "not free" overlook the fact that Russia has less widespread poverty than the US and China.[325] To this end, although government corruption in Russia contributes to holes in its infrastructure, one must consider that its system of governance is economically sound.

The Russian Federation operates and regulates the ideal socialist market-based economy. Russia's government has successfully balanced socialism in heavy state intervention in business, banking, and investment with liberal economic policies such as increased privatization of business. Property rights could be extended in the private sector a bit more, but Russia will easily adapt to the socioeconomic revolution. My advice to Russia is to maintain the status quo—things are working just fine.

Ukraine

Ukraine has maintained independence since the dissolution of the Soviet Union in 1991. It is struggling to recover from the global economic crisis, which "triggered a significant recession"[326]:

> The drop in steel prices and Ukraine's exposure to the global financial crisis due to aggressive foreign borrowing lowered growth in 2008 and the economy contracted more than 15% in 2009, among the worst economic performances in the world.[327]

Not surprisingly, Ukraine is looking to Russia for support:

> In January 2010, Victor Yanukovych of the Party of Regions was elected the country's fifth president. Since gaining power, Yanukovych has fast-tracked rapprochement with Russia.[328]

Poverty and corruption are endemic. The Heritage Foundation gave Ukraine a failing grade of 45.8/100. Ukraine needs to improve laws governing investment regulations and protection of private property. Reduction of corruption is the first step to improving Ukraine's economy.

Conclusion

Europe is characterized by extreme levels of inequity and persistent corruption. The economic and political struggles of Europe offer a glimpse into the future of other world nations that are currently developing.

CHAPTER 6

Drugs in the Americas

Money laundering and the production and trafficking of narcotics, although a worldwide phenomenon, are particularly endemic in Central and South America. As a result of narcotrafficking, organized crime and corruption represent permanent obstacles to economic freedom in most of the countries of Central and South America. This is because much labor and money is poured into, and laundered from, the production of illicit drugs. As a result of money laundering kleptocracies, widespread poverty and malnourishment are becoming crises in Central and South America, particularly in Bolivia and Guatemala.

New Regulations for Controlled Substances

New Regulations for controlled drugs would allow narcotrafficking countries to increase production of said drugs, thus providing poverty-stricken countries with an additional source of agricultural income. The 1961, 1971, and 1988 UN Drug Conventions should be revised to strictly enforce regulation of these drugs, much in the same way alcohol and tobacco are regulated. National laws in Central and South America must follow suit so that free, legal drugs can be exported to the world market. There can, however, be discrepancies in state law that place further restrictions on narcotics.

Argentina

Argentina has many strong points such as low unemployment and a strong economy, yet it also has several weaknesses, such as widespread poverty and corruption. From the Heritage Foundation's 2011 report: "Institutional weaknesses, including corruption and a weak judiciary, continue to hold back Argentina's overall economic freedom and development".[329] Human trafficking is an ongoing issue in Argentina. From the US Department of State's 2010 report: "Bolivians, Paraguayans, and Peruvians, as well as Colombians and Dominicans, are subjected to forced labor in sweatshops, on farms, and increasingly in grocery stores and as street vendors."[330] Although Argentina doesn't produce many narcotics, it is an "important" transit route for illegal substances.[331] The country's president, Cristina Fernandez de Kirchner, has tried to pass an anti-corruption bill; if it does not pass, Argentina will be considered a money laundering country. If illegal substances are "legalized", it might be possible for Argentina to avoid the embarrassment of attaining the money laundering label.

Bolivia

Bolivia, a self-proclaimed Socialist Unitarian State, is one of the poorest countries in South America. 20-34% of its population of 10 million is malnourished. There is significant narcotics production in Bolivia:

> Bolivia is the world's third largest cocaine producer and a significant transit zone for Peruvian-origin cocaine. Bolivia also produces marijuana, primarily for domestic consumption. Existing reports indicate that most Bolivian-origin cocaine flows to other Latin American countries, especially Brazil, for domestic consumption or onward transit towards Europe, with little exported to the United States.[332]

Although the government is committed to eliminating production of coca, it is nevertheless legal to chew the naturally occurring plant, and government regulations strive to permit use of the substance. Evo Morales, the current president, is a supporter of coca chewing:

> Bolivian President Evo Morales is also president of the coca growers' federation in the Chapare region of Bolivia, one of the two major coca-growing areas. In 2010, the GOB continued efforts to amend the 1961 Single Convention on Narcotic Drugs by removing references to coca leaf chewing. The GOB also remained committed to passing legislation raising the legal number of hectares of coca cultivation from 12,000 to 20,000 hectares. The Morales Administration maintained its "social control" policy for illicit coca eradication in which the GOB negotiates with coca growers to obtain their consent for eradication. In 2010, eradication forces

met resistance from coca growers, including large protests, road blockades, and stone throwing, forcing the GOB to temporarily withdraw eradication forces from Palos Blancos and Carrasco National Park.[333]

Movement Towards Socialism

The Movement Towards Socialism (MAS), the majority party of Bolivia, is pushing the country politically in the right direction. MAS needs to ensure that its investment and business laws are clearly understood in order to consolidate socialism in Bolivia most effectively. Regarding property rights:

Article 308 of the 2009 constitution states that "the private accumulation of economic power" will not be permitted to "endanger the economic sovereignty of the State" and that the "the right to own private property either individually or collectively [must] fulfill a social function" and "not harm the collective interest." Although other statutes guarantee property rights, the judicial process is subject to political influence and corruption.[334]

These revisions might not sound appealing to foreign investors, however, since Bolivia has a fair amount of natural resources, it is certainly possible for its centralized government to make a few concessions for business entrepreneurs.

Conclusion

My prediction is that MAS will allow greater foreign investment in the next decade, and will continue to reform government regulations in such a way as to balance state control of businesses with increased stakes for foreign investors. I wholeheartedly support Morales' support of coca growing and suggest that fully legalized cultivation of the plant might be more beneficial to Bolivia's economy.

Brazil

Brazil, the world's fifth largest country, is the economic heavyweight of South America—not surprisingly, "corruption is significant".[335] The country ranked 69 in Transparency International's 2010 Corruption Perceptions Index, making it an average-level country of corruption. Money laundering is an ongoing concern in Brazil; its sources include "domestic crime, especially drug trafficking . . . organized crime, gambling, and trade in various types of contraband."[336] Brazil has several issues to deal with in addition to corruption, including weak laws, forced labor, and widespread poverty.

On property rights and the judiciary of Brazil:

> Contracts are generally considered secure, but Brazil's judiciary is inefficient, subject to political and economic influence, and lacks resources and staff training. Decisions can take years, and judgments by the Supreme Federal Tribunal are not automatically binding on lower courts.

Bureaucracy and administration are non-transparent, burdensome, complex, and subject to corruption. Businesses bidding on government procurement contracts can encounter corruption, which is also a problem in the lower courts. Corruption can be an obstacle to investment.[337]

Poverty and Forced Labor

A 2008 estimate places Brazil's level of poverty at 26%.[338] According to Plan, a worldwide children's development organization, "22 million children live below the poverty line in families who live on less than $2 per day."[339] According to the US Department of State's 2010 Report on Human Trafficking, there are 25,000 Brazilians used for slave labor on cattle ranches, logging and mining camps, sugarcane plantations, and various farms. Laborers from Bolivia, Paraguay, and China are persuaded to find work in Sao Paulo textile sweatshops with the false notion that they will be fairly compensated.[340] Needless to say, the slave and sweatshop labor is unacceptable and must be addressed immediately.

Conclusion

Trying to solve Brazil's problems of corruption and ineffective judiciary is a bit like David going up against Goliath. There are many governments and NGO's who already are tackling the various issues that directly affect Brazil's economy, and I have nothing further to add to their suggestions. That being said, Brazil could easily adapt to most of my socio-economic ideas.

Colombia

Colombiaisadrugcountry. Inequality, underemployment, and narcotrafficking remain significant impediments to overhauling its basic infrastructure and reducing poverty that affects nearly half of its populace.[341] Already hundreds of millions of US dollars and billions of Colombian pesos have been spent on the endless drug war. Although Colombia is a "regional leader" in the fight against illegal narcotics, the "laundering of money from Colombia's illicit cocaine and heroin trade continues to penetrate its economy and affect its financial institutions".[342] According to the US Department of State:

> The United States has designated three illegal armed groups in Colombia as Foreign Terrorist Organizations (FTOs). The Revolutionary Armed Forces of Colombia (FARC), the now demobilized United Self-Defense Forces (AUC) and, to a lesser degree, the Army of Liberation (ELN) exercise considerable influence over areas with high concentrations of coca and opium poppy cultivation.[343] These FTOs used drug cultivation and trafficking proceeds to wage war on the government resulting in high levels of violence, displacement, economic stagnation, and insecurity.[344]

At this time, the FARC and other FTO's pose the greatest threat to the impoverished communities in Colombia. Thousands of children have been "forcibly" recruited into armed guerilla factions, and many communities have been displaced.[345] Moreover, "children are subjected to forced labor in mines and quarries or as domestic servants".[346] For instance, in March 2011 alone, "at least 800 ethnic Afro-Colombians have had to flee their homes in western Colombia . . . because of a struggle between armed groups in the mineral-rich area to control illegal mining activities".[347] Gangs and organized criminal networks force their relatives, acquaintances, and displaced persons "into conditions of forced prostitution and forced labor, including forced work in the illegal drug trade".[348]

Conclusion

It is unlikely that significant social progress will be achieved in Colombia, since corruption is so pervasive: "Despite notable improvements in fighting corruption and narcotics trafficking, concerns remain over the influence of criminal organizations on the police, the military, and lower levels of the judiciary and civil service".[349] Government corruption is the largest obstacle to economic freedom in Colombia. Therefore, cocaine production should be "legalized" in Colombia in order to "reduce" government corruption and end the drug war.

Costa Rica

From the US Department of State: "While Costa Rica is not a major regional financial center, it remains vulnerable to money laundering and other financial crimes. Illicit proceeds from fraud, trafficking in persons, arms, narcotics trafficking (mainly cocaine), and corruption are laundered in Costa Rica."[350] The amount of people living below poverty level in Costa Rica has increased 5.7% between 2006 and 2009.[351] [352] Moreover, according to the US Department of State, there is an increased incidence of forced labor in the country.[353] Corruption is the greatest threat to freedom in Costa Rica:

> The government does not emphasize enforcement of anti-corruption laws, regulations, and penalties. Allegations of lower-level corruption are common, and some prosecutions have resulted. Some foreign firms complain of corruption in the administration of public tenders.[354]

Anti-corruption measures in Costa Rica could slowly be spiraling out of control if strict enforcement is not upheld. Costa Rica is obviously fucked, but legalization of cocaine might just be the lube it's looking for.

Dominican Republic

The United States of America has great responsibility for the Dominican Republic, since we are its largest investors. Although the country has stable economic growth, corruption remains a problem. As with many other countries in Central America, money laundering is an ongoing issue, and "the lack of a single recognized financial intelligence unit exacerbates the problem".[355] A proposal for an offshore financial center "may worsen the DR's vulnerability to money laundering".[356] According to research conducted by the Heritage Foundation: "Despite recent reforms, Dominican and foreign business leaders complain that judicial and administrative corruption affects the settlement of business disputes."[357]

Endemic corruption obviously affects more than foreign investment, as poverty and hunger are both widespread in the Dominican Republic. A 2007 World Bank estimate places 48.5% of Dominicans below the poverty line; more than 2 million of them are going hungry based on a report by the Nations United Agency for Nutrition Assistance.[358]

Solutions

In the course of my research, I came across an interesting proposed solution to end hunger. With the recent introduction of many edible fish into its waters, the Dominican Republic should invest in fish farming if it wants to create a controllable and sustainable source of food. State investments must be made to remove contaminants from the Dominican Republic's freshwater (this should be a priority even if fish farming is not implemented). The priority for the Dominican Republic is, however, to address ongoing corruption.

Ecuador

Widespread poverty, malnourishment and low unemployment are all endemic to Ecuador. From the CIA: "Economic policies under the Correa administration—including an announcement in late 2009 of its intention to terminate 13 bilateral investment treaties, including one with the United States—have generated economic uncertainty and discouraged private investment."[359] Moreover, narcotrafficking is endemic: "Sandwiched between Colombia and Peru and bordering the Pacific Ocean on the west, Ecuador is a major transit country for cocaine and heroin."[360]

Obviously diplomacy in foreign relations is not Correa's strong suit. This corrupt country could be a prime candidate for legalization of drug production, which would help to provide transparency of funds.

El Salvador

El Salvador is a transit country for cocaine and other narcotics shipped from South America, and although there are no sources that reveal specific evidence of money laundering, it is very likely that this is a part of low-level bureaucratic corruption. For instance, in 2008, El Salvador's national police chief stepped down amidst allegations of corruption and links with drug trafficking.[361] Finance Minister Carlos Cáceres opened a commission to investigate corruption within former President Antonio Saca's government in 2009. Specific allegations of fraud included "ghost employees" on payroll at the National Registry Centre, as well as other offices.[362] In the 2011 Index of Economic Freedom, the Heritage Foundation implied that there may be pervasive bribery within El Salvador's bureaucracy, and gave the country a failing grade for freedom from corruption. Property rights are poorly protected as a result of corruption, and most likely as a result of poor legislation as well.[363] Until corruption is rooted out, the 38% of Salvadorians living below the poverty line will continue to suffer political and economic injustices.

Guatemala

Guatemala's GDP is roughly half that of the other countries in Central America. 8% of the population lives in extreme poverty and 20-34% of the population suffers from malnourishment.[364] There are still a million internally displaced persons as a result of over 30 years of civil war.[365] Forced labor is an ongoing problem in Guatemala, "particularly near the border with Mexico", and indigenous Guatemalans are "particularly vulnerable to labor exploitation".[366] Although there are no details available, my guess is that some of this forced labor is in some way connected to organized crime.

Guatemala is the "epicenter" of Central American narcotics trafficking, since "its geographic location makes it an ideal haven for transnational organized crime groups, including human and drug trafficking organizations".[367] It is an important "transshipment route for South American cocaine and heroin destined for the United States and for returning cash to South America".[368] Unfortunately, there may be an uptick in violence in Guatemala's future, since "the narcotics trade is increasingly linked to arms trafficking".[369]

Unfortunately, it will be difficult for Guatemala to pursue further industrialization and improve its infrastructure since it lacks essential resources aside from small reserves of petroleum. The poor people in Guatemala depend heavily on agriculture—coffee and sugar provide the country with most of its export-earned GDP. If production and distribution of narcotics were encouraged in this country, it would boost both agricultural exports and the services-based sector of Guatemala's economy, thus improving employment and the raising the standard of living for indigenous Guatemalans.

Haiti

Haiti has dealt with much internal strife and political corruption since gaining independence in 1804. Unfortunately, as a result of its history of revolt, decades of punitive sanctions in the 20th century, and continuing corruption, it remains the poorest country in the western hemisphere. The first democratic elections took place in 2006 with the help of UN and US involvement, however, there are holes in Haiti's legislative and judiciary branches.

Corruption is "rampant" in Haiti, and although international donors have called for reforms, little has been done to improve Haiti's outdated laws or root out institutionalized corruption.[370] Specific problems include bribery (customs officers), and smuggling of contraband (small arms and narcotics), which "accounts for a large percentage of the manufactured consumables market".[371] Most troubling of all is the severe lack of property rights in Haiti. According to the Heritage Foundation: "Most commercial disputes are settled out of court if at all. Widespread corruption allows disputing parties to purchase favorable outcomes. Real property interests are handicapped by the absence of a comprehensive civil registry".[372] Unfortunately, "despite improving financial intelligence and enforcement capacity, the weakness of the Haitian judicial system and prosecutorial mechanism continues to leave the country vulnerable to corruption and money laundering".[373]

Haiti's crises

Haiti's 2010 earthquake severely "impacted all aspects of Haitian life" and created negative "ripple effects in the banking, commercial and criminal justice institutions".[374]

The devastating 7.0 earthquake will cost the country at least $7.8 billion dollars[375], and although much of its debt was canceled, Haiti has already racked up another $400 million in new debt.[376] Haiti's "formal labor market is not fully developed"—the 2010 earthquake only worsened this situation—currently a large portion of the workforce is unemployed.[377] 80% of Haiti's population lives on $1-2 per day[378] according to the CIA (2003 est.), although this figure probably should be adjusted considering that the figures are outdated. Disease is fairly rampant in Haiti, particularly HIV, which afflicts about 2% of the adult population. Moreover, a cholera outbreak in 2010 has infected thousands of Haitians.

Solutions

Although Eurasian Minerals Inc. and Newmont Mining Co. signed a joint-venture to speculate for gold in Haiti[379], there is otherwise a general lack of investment in Haiti, which is an oversight. Haiti's economy is primarily dependent upon agriculture and textiles, which is curious considering that there are unused reserves of bauxite, copper, minerals containing calcium carbonate, gold and potential reserves of oil as well. If new ventures were opened up in Haiti's mining sector, this would create new training and jobs for Haitians, thus lifting some of its population out of extreme poverty. This best solution to put Haiti on the track to improving its Human Development, and joining the global community on a more equal footing. If Haiti pursues this path, it must require that mining operations follow international environmental standards, thereby avoiding situations such as the pollution debacle in the Dominican Republic.

Substantial reduction of corruption in Haiti must obviously precede such ventures, as accountability and transparency are essential to creating and maintaining foreign investment partnerships. If Haiti revises its legislative and judiciary branches of government as needed, foreign countries will begin to take interest in investing in Haiti's dire political-economic situation. Once these revisions take place, Haiti can focus on rebuilding its devastated infrastructure in order to create a sustainable economy.

Honduras

From the CIA: "Honduras, the second poorest country in Central America, suffers from extraordinarily unequal distribution of income, as well as high underemployment."[380] Similar to El Salvador, there is narcotics trafficking, but no documented money laundering. According to the US Department of State: "Corruption within the Honduran government and its law enforcement elements presents obstacles to counter-narcotics efforts."[381] Honduras ranked abysmally (25/100) in Freedom from Corruption on Transparency International's Corruption Perceptions Index for 2010. Corruption is "pervasive in government procurement, government permits, and land titling".[382]

As luck would have it, Honduras is fairly rich in minerals. As with so many other countries, mining negligence is an issue. Hondurans have already spoken out against the mining companies' mistreatment of indigenous people; now they can have a say in how these mining companies exploit their land. My proposal is that Honduras follow a similar path to the one I've outlaid for Haiti. Similarly, eradication of corruption in the government is a necessary precursor to establish a system of checks and balances to regulate companies, which are often "selectively" negligent of international environmental laws.

Jamaica

Jamaica's economy is mostly based upon services, with tourism accounting for about 10% of its GDP. Jamaica is, however, dealing with an "onerous debt burden"; it is the fourth highest in the world on a per capita basis.[383] The drug war, in conjunction with debt, only adds to Jamaica's significant budget deficit:

> The Golding administration faces the difficult prospect of having to achieve fiscal discipline in order to maintain debt payments, while simultaneously attacking a serious crime problem that is hampering economic growth. High unemployment exacerbates the crime problem, including gang violence that is fueled by the drug trade.[384]

The Finance Minister of Jamaica said that the country is "seeking $1 billion in loans and grants to rid the country of 'cancerous' drug gangs that have taken over poor neighborhoods on the Caribbean island and hurt economic growth."[385] So far, this economic paradigm has worked well for Jamaica, since it depends on loans just as any other developed country and especially considering that "Jamaica continues to be the largest Caribbean supplier of marijuana to the United States."[386]. There is, however, a much better paradigm that will reduce debt burden in Jamaica:

> Legalize marijuana and standardize regulations of its use in accordance with the guidelines I've laid out for the United States of America. Legalization of marijuana production, distribution and use of marijuana will reduce some of the corruption in Jamaica, abate drug related crimes, stop the war on drugs, and ultimately reduce debt burden in Jamaica.

Mexico·

Mexico is a very wealthy country, yet there is a tremendous money gap leaving 47% of the population in poverty.[387] This undoubtedly has much to do with Mexico's ongoing issues with money laundering:

> Corruption has been pervasive for years, and most Mexican external audit institutions lack operational and budgetary independence. President Calderon has committed his administration to fight against corruption at all levels of government and in 2008 launched Operación Limpieza, investigating and imprisoning corrupt government officials in enforcement agencies.[388]

The corruption of corrupt government officials in the enforcement agencies is irrefutably linked to drug cartels and money laundering:

Mexico is both a major transit and source country for illicit drugs reaching the United States. Approximately 95 percent of the estimated cocaine flow toward the United States transits the Mexico-Central America corridor from its origins in South America. Mexico is also a major supplier of heroin, marijuana, and methamphetamine to the United States. Other significant sources of illegal proceeds being laundered include corruption, kidnapping, and trafficking in firearms and persons.[389]

Mexico's drug wars have killed 35,000 since 2006, and there is no sign that it will stop anytime soon. According to the Guardian, "Killings reached their highest level in 2010, when there were 15,273 deaths, up from 9,616 the previous year."[390] Former president Vicente Fox has been a vocal supporter of legalization and taxation of production, sales, and distribution of "illicit" drugs.[391] According to Fox, prohibition never works: "Prohibition didn't work in the Garden of Eden. Adam ate the apple."[392]

Conclusion

Legalization of all drug production and distribution in Mexico would end the drug wars, reduce violent crime, reduce kidnappings, reduce money laundering, and create greater transparency in the Mexican government. This in turn would also help to close the poverty gap. If Mexico initiated legalization, a trickle-down economic effect would be felt in parts of Central and South America.

Who would operate the production facilities and oversee distribution? The answer to this question is quite simple. The drug kingpins should be allowed to continue operating their businesses as usual, with one crucial difference: they would need to be regulated by Mexican government as well.

Panama

Panama has a high percentage of employment, especially compared to the rest of Central America, yet a quarter of its population still lives in poverty. This undoubtedly is partly influenced by its eastern neighbor Colombia. From the US Department of State:

> Panama's strategic geographic location and its economic openness make it a natural location for laundering money derived from drug sales. However, location is only one reason for Panama's attractiveness for money launderers. Panama is promoting itself as the new hub for Central America because it is a leader in developing the physical and financial infrastructure that go with that role. The Colon Free Trade Zone is the second largest free trade zone in the world and the major airline, Copa, is expanding international and local flights. The financial sector is increasing direct marketing efforts to attract regional financial institutions. This current and future access to infrastructure and global connections attracts international clients who know how

to use financial and commercial accounts
for money laundering.[393]

Clearly, Panama's convenient location and financial
resources make it a prime candidate for legalization of
"illicit" drugs. Unfortunately, money laundering is also
convenient, so legalization seems quite unlikely. Thus,
Panama's poor will ultimately remain the losers in all of
this, unless Mexico decides to go legal.

Paraguay

Paraguay is a major producer of soy and cannabis.
Cannabis should be legalized and exploited immediately if
Paraguay is to make improvements in its agricultural sector.
From the US Department of State: "Paraguay is a major drug
transit country and money laundering center."[394] As with
most countries on this list, corruption remains an obstacle
to improving the economy. Legalization of cannabis would
"reduce" corruption.

Peru

Due to government corruption and greed, malnourishment
is reaching epidemic proportions in Peru, a nation that is
struggling to become middle-class. It is a major source of
money laundering and narcotics trafficking:

> Peru is the world's second-largest
> producer of cocaine and, according to U.S.
> Government (USG) statistics, in 2009 had
> an estimated 40,000 hectares (ha) used
> for coca cultivation nationwide. Cocaine
> is transported over land to neighboring

countries, and to Europe, the Far East, Mexico, the Caribbean, and the United States via maritime conveyances and commercial air flights. Peru is also a major importer of precursor chemicals used for cocaine production.[395]

7% of Peru's cultivation of coca leaf is legal. If there were 100% legalization of coca leaf cultivation, Peru's overall GDP from agriculture and services could be increased.

Venezuela

Under the auspices of Hugo Chávez's social democracy, Venezuela has become one of the most corrupt countries in South America. The Chávez oligarchy has neglected the needs of the public sector, which has led to a growing dissatisfaction in the country. Much of Venezuela's corruption is well publicized, but I will summarize it again here.

An article on Chávez' government appeared in a March 2008 issue of USA Today, in which its corruption was laid out in detail. Notable examples of grand corruption included: Chávez' acceptance of foreign contributions for his presidential campaign after his election, and offering Ponzi deals to political leaders and countries.[396] "Many of the promises never will be fulfilled, but . . . expenditures and promises have been made directly by Chávez, without consulting the people of Venezuela or following normal administrative procedures."[397] Of particular interest is that many of these deals were made in order to secure "acquisitions of about $6,000,000,000 worth of sophisticated weaponry from Russia, China, Belarus, and other countries."[398]

Examples of bureaucratic corruption include: public contracting without bids for over a decade, and corruption at the National Electorate Council.[399] Between 2005-2008, 2 million voters were added to the electoral registry—this is statistically impossible, revolution or not. "Still worse, these voters have no proper addresses or reliable identities, making them 'virtual' voters that could be used by the government to swing any election."[400]

Oil Corruption

A new oil deal with China has been in international news recently. Venezuela's PDVSA (Petroleos de Venezuela) and China's CITIC Group for mining and drilling have signed a new deal in which China has agreed to invest $4 billion dollars in housing for Venezuela's capital, Caracas.[401] Notable deals between Venezuela and China include "Caracas' purchase of 18 Chinese K-8 fighter jets, and assistance to launch a telecommunications satellite."[402] The PDVSA is expecting China to invest $40 billion over the next six years.[403] This investment is the best thing that could possibly happen for Venezuela, despite the fact that China's foreign mining practices are anything but reputable, as we learned earlier.

Chinese corruption aside, the PDVSA is guilty of institutionalized corruption in its own right. For instance, PDVSA pension funds were used in a Ponzi scheme run by former financial advisor Francisco Illaramendi, who allegedly "juggled 100's of millions of dollars between hedge funds" and misappropriated approximately $53 million from a fund he personally managed.[404] In June 2010, PDVAL, a subsidiary of the PDVSA[405], admitted to letting 30,000 tons of food rot in the docks during a food crisis[406] (for security reasons), although outside estimates place the total amount of rotted food at 75,000 tons.[407] Food shortages caused extreme inflation, and this trend has continued; for instance, from January to March 2011 inflation reached 28.7%.[408] Fortunately, extreme inflation will not be a problem anymore after the worldwide economic revolution since food will be free.

Housing & Electricity Crisis

Venezuela's housing crisis is exacerbated by lackadaisical government policy and corruption in general. There are over 2 million houses needed for its population of 28 million; slow progress and environmental disasters have been major setbacks.[409] Housing and Habitat Minister Ricardo Molina claims the government "aims to build 150,000 homes in 2011" and Chávez set 2017 as the end-date goal for completion of 2 million homes.[410] Critics of Chávez cite lack of progress in the housing projects due to widespread government seizures and mismanagement.[411] This is hard to refute considering how slowly the program has progressed despite the fact that the 2011 housing budget is a mere $480 million[412] and especially considering that China just offered to invest $4 billion in Venezuela's housing. The solution to Venezuela's housing crisis just might require Venezuelans to accept an age-old adage—better late than never.

As if this wasn't enough, Venezuela also suffered from blackouts in 2010 due to electricity shortages. Many critics blame the government for not making thermoelectric power plants fully operational, which is a valid criticism, since the plants only account for 30% of the country's electric supply.[413] Venezuela needs to invest in more thermoelectric energy if it hopes to withstand severe droughts, as was the case in 2010, so that it is not dependent upon its hydroelectric dams. Fortunately, this seems to be the case, since Sidor (Venezuela's steel company) has plans to make its first thermoelectric plant in Venezuela fully operational later in 2011.

Human Trafficking

Migrants from Colombia, Peru, and China are subjected to forced labor, particularly in the Orinoco River Basin area and the border regions of Tachira State, where victims are exploited in mining operations.[414] There is also considerable political violence between Venezuela's military and Colombian right wing paramilitary units and leftist rebel groups infiltrating through the border.[415] Obviously Chávez needs to address this problem in accordance with The US Department of State.

Illicit Drug Trade & Money Laundering

While all of this is troubling, the icing on the cake is Venezuela's involvement in money laundering and narcotics trafficking. According to the US Dept of State: "Money laundering occurs through commercial banks, exchange houses, gambling sites, fraudulently invoiced foreign trade transactions, smuggling, real estate (in the tourist industry), agriculture and livestock businesses, securities transactions, and trade in precious metals".[416] Drug trafficking is Venezuela's main source of money laundering. The United Nations' 2010 World Drug Report revealed that between 2006 and 2008, over half the detected maritime shipments of cocaine to Europe came through Venezuela.

Cocaine is also "trafficked through Venezuela to the Eastern Caribbean, Central America, the United States, Europe, and western Africa".[417] Venezuela is now "one of the principal drug-transit countries in the Western Hemisphere."[418] From an article in USA Today:

> Drug smuggling through Venezuela has exploded since President Hugo Chávez severed contacts with U.S. law enforcement agencies in 2005, U.S. and United Nations officials say in reports. The extent of Chávez's involvement in the drug trade is in question. He has been seizing businesses and prodding Latin nations to turn to socialism as his regime grapples with a significant loss of revenue tied to the drop in the price of Venezuela's main legal export: oil.[419]

It is unlikely that the Venezuela's status as a transit country for illegal narcotics will change anytime soon. In fact, outside organizations may be priming Venezuela to become a producer of these drugs as well. For instance, "in 2010, Mexican drug trafficking organizations gained an increased presence in Venezuela".[420] The involvement of Venezuela's military and corrupt bureaucrats in the drug trade, combined with the growing presence of the Colombian cartel suggests that future production of illicit drugs within Venezuela is not an entirely unlikely scenario.

Conclusion

As a result of corruption and negligence, unemployment and poverty remain uncomfortably high in Venezuela. Nearly a third of its population lives below the poverty line of $1.25 per day, and unemployment is rising at an alarming rate; currently 12% of the population is unemployed.[421] Hopefully Chávez, who has essentially become a dictator, can get his country back on track. In the long run, I think Venezuela is bound to succeed economically under Chávez. What we are witnessing is growing pains as Venezuela continues to expand its service-based sector and struggles to reform its steel industry. Furthermore, I have confidence that Chávez will better regulate PDVSA and PDVAL so that the company operates at maximum efficiency. Venezuela's politics make it a prime candidate for my socio-economic agenda.

To Conclude

Narcotics trafficking and money laundering undoubtedly exacerbate government corruption in Central and South America by providing a source of revenue for which crooked officials have no need to provide accountability. Furthermore, so long as the demand for cocaine and heroin remain high in North America, Europe and Western Africa, crooked security forces and other officials will continue to aid drug producers in providing a consistent supply to the world market. From this perspective, the "war" on drugs is merely a sideshow so that Central and South American governments can keep up appearances since there really is no incentive to completely eliminate the illegal narcotics trade.

Bringing narcotics production "out of the closet" will improve both the economy and the standard of living for Central and South America. The drug wars—which have cost the international community billions of dollars and killed hundreds of thousands—will be ended. Economic benefits for the Americas would include:

1. Increased privatization of the illicit drugs industry.
2. Increased competition in the production and distribution of illicit drugs.
3. Increased competition in "drug awareness" and "drug safety" marketing and advertising.
4. Increased labor in the agricultural sector.

Not all nations need agree upon revised UN Drug Conventions but they must agree to respect the sovereignty of nations who do agree to the revisions. In this way, narcotics can be "legal" in some nations, and not others. By "legalizing" and regulating illicit drugs, the governments of Central and South America can provide better transparency and accountability for narcotics related revenues. Until controlled substances enjoy greater legalization in Central and South America, with appropriate regulations under revised UN Drug Conventions, many indigenous people in Central and South America will continue to suffer in rural poverty.

ENDNOTES

Chapter 2: Asia

1 CIA-The World Factbook.
2 *Ibid.*
3 *Ibid.*
4 The Heritage Foundation; 2011 Index of Economic Freedom.
5 *Ibid.*
6 *One World South Asia*; "Millions turn landless in Bangladesh"; 9, Jun 2010.
7 *Ibid.*
8 Land Law; *Land Reform Ordinance*; Sec. 7.
9 Paul van der Molen and Arbind Man Tuladhar; "Corruption and Land Administration"; *International Federation of Surveyors Article of the Month*; March 2007.
10 *The Daily Star*; "Bangladesh betters on hunger challenge"; 18 Oct, 2010.
11 CIA- The World Factbook.
12 Human Rights Watch: World Report 2011.
13 Wikipedia; Ratanakiri Province.
14 The CIA Factbook; China.
15 *Ibid.*
16 Seth Faison, "A Roar of Silent Protesters." New York Times, 27 Apr, 1999.
17 Leeshai Lemish, "How China is Silencing Falun Gong," National Post 7 Oct, 2008.

18 U.S. Department of State, 2009 Country Report on Human Rights: China (includes Hong Kong and Macao).

19 Falun Dafa; Clearwisdom.net; 4 Aug, 2004.

20 Kilgour, David; Bloody Harvest; Revised Report into Allegations of Organ Harvesting of Falun Gong Practitioners in China; B; 31 Jan, 2007.

21 Laogai Research Foundation; Death Penalty & Organ Harvesting; www.laogai.org.

22 Kilgour, David; Bloody Harvest; Revised Report into Allegations of Organ Harvesting of Falun Gong Practitioners in China; 31 Jan, 2007.

23 Wu, Hongda Harry. Laogai - The Chinese Gulag. Boulder, CO: Westview Press, Inc., 1992. Print.

24 Laogai Research Foundation; www.laogai.org.

25 Laogai Museum press release; 23 Mar, 2009.

26 Free Tibetan Heroes; org2.democracyinaction.org; article: "Release Dhondup Wangchen!"

27 Laogai Research Foundation; www.laogai.org.

28 Laogai Research Foundation; www.laogai.com.

29 Razmy, Austin; *Time*; New Report Released on China's Black Jails, 12 Nov, 2009.

30 *Ibid.*

31 Zhang, Tao; "Media Control and Self-censorship in Hong Kong"; *Trend*; Nov 2006.

32 Xiang, Zhang; news.xinhuanet.com; 27 Oct, 2010.

33 *Ibid.*

34 *Ibid.*

35 The World Food Programme.

36 Guardian.co.uk; "Two Million Slum Children Die Every Year as India Booms"; 4 Oct, 2009.

37 *Times of India*; "45,000 Child Malnutrition Deaths Every Yr in Maharasthra"; 4 Feb, 2010.

38 Wikipedia; Palagummi Sainath.

39 India Together; "Attaining Food Security by Definition"; P. Sainath; 5 Sep, 2010.

40 *Ibid.*

41 Countercurrents.org; "Systemic Starvation in Melghat"; Shirish Khare; 4 Feb, 2011.

42 Time and Us: Starvation Deaths in Maharasthra; posted by anu, 21 Sep, 2008.

43 Sanhati; "Adivasis, Mining and Monopoly Capital": *Issue 18 of Update Booklet*; 4 May 2010; pgs.65-68.

44 *The Financial Express*: "Jharkhand's Ecological Predators on the Prowl", 19 Mar, 2011.

45 Sanhati; "Adivasis, Mining and Monopoly Capital": *Issue 18 of Update Booklet*; 4 May, 2010; pg.35.

46 Gits4u.com: "Large Scale Illegal Mining in India", 2010.

47 Human Rights Watch: World Report 2011.

48 Sanhati; "Adivasis, Mining and Monopoly Capital": *Issue 18 of Update Booklet*; 4 May 2010; pgs.65-68.; pgs.11-17.

49 ChannelnewsAsia.com; "Sembcorp's Newater plant…"; 18 Jun, 2009.

50 *The Times (London)*; "India Looks to the Sun for Ambitious Surge in Green Power"; 3 Aug, 2009; Page, Jeremy.

51 World Bank; Empowering Rural India: Expanding Electricity Access by Mobilizing Local Resources; 2010; Pg. 11.

52 CIA-The World Factbook.

53 The World Food Programme.

54 The Heritage Foundation: 2011 Index of Economic Freedom.

55 Ridwan Max Sijabat and Bagus Saragih; "Political corruption in Indonesia reaches alarming level"; *The Jakarta Post*; 31 Jan, 2011.

56 Shonhardt, Sarah; "Wikileaks tie Indonesia's President to Corruption"; *Huffpost World;* 14 Mar 2011.

57 The Heritage Foundation: 2011 Index of Economic Freedom.

58   *Ibid.*

59   Human Rights Watch: World Report 2011.

60   *Ibid.*

61   *Ibid.*

62   CIA-The World Factbook.

63   MacKinnon, Ian; "40 years on Laos reaps bitter harvest of the secret war"; *The Guardian;* 3 Dec 2008.

64   US Dept of State; Report on Human Trafficking, 2010.

65   *Ibid.*

66   *Republica*; "China eyes Nepal's mining sector"; 9 Aug, 2009.

67   CIA-The World Factbook.

68   The Heritage Foundation: 2011 Index of Economic Freedom.

69   Uriminzokkiri.com; Juche.

70   Constitution of North Korea (1972; Preamble).

71   Constitution of North Korea (1972; Article 40).

72   Brooke, James; "North Korea, Facing Food Shortages, Mobilizes Millions From the Cities to Help Rice Farmers"; *The New York Times*; 1 Jun, 2005.

73   Lee, Jong-Heon; "China's Economic Support of N Korea Undermines US led Sanctions"; spacewar.com; 13 Feb, 2006.

74   Wikipedia; Human Rights in North Korea.

75   "North Korea slashes food rations"; *BBC News*; 24 Jan, 2005.

76   So-Hyun, Kim; "North Korea seeks rice, fertilizer aid from Seoul"; *The Korea Herald*; 28 Oct, 2010.

77   US Dept of State; Country Reports on Human Rights Practices; May 2006.

78   "North Korean human trafficking thrives across N Korea-China border"; *Chosun*; reliefweb.int 3 Mar, 2008.

79   UN Human Rights Resolution 2005/11; 14 Apr, 2005.

80 Willacy, Mark; "North Korean women being sold as sex slaves in China"; *ABC*; 22 Oct, 2010.

81 Hawk, David; *The Hidden Gulag*; US Committee for Human Rights in North Korea, 2004, p. 56.

82 *Ibid.*

83 *Ibid.*

84 *Ibid.*

85 *Ibid;* p. 24.

86 *Ibid.*

87 *Ibid;* pp. 69-72.

88 Harden, Blaine; "North Korean Prison Camp Escapee Tells of Horrors, Worries About Those Left Behind"; *The Washington Post*; 11 Dec, 2008.

89 Barnett, Anthony; "Revealed; the gas chamber horror of North Korea's gulag"; *The Observer*; 1 Feb, 2004.

90 Human Rights Commission, New York; 2004; awomansvoice. org.

91 Barnett, Anthony; "Revealed; the gas chamber horror of North Korea's gulag"; *The Observer*; 1 Feb, 2004.

92 English-pravda.ru; "North Korea resumes public executions"; 26 Nov, 2007.

93 Amnesty International / Australia; "Public executions by North Korea is another injustice"; 7 Mar, 2008.

94 Human Rights Commission, New York; 2004; awomansvoice. org.

95 English-pravda.ru: "North Korea resumes public executions"; 26 Nov, 2007.

96 The Heritage Foundation: 2011 Index of Economic Freedom.

97 *Ibid.*

98 Hawk, David; *The Hidden Gulag*; US Committee for Human Rights in North Korea, 2004, p. 42.

99 The Heritage Foundation: 2011 Index of Economic Freedom.

100 US Dept of State: 2011 International Narcotics Control Strategy Report (INCSR).

101 CIA-The World Factbook.

102 The Heritage Foundation: 2011 Index of Economic Freedom.

103 *Ibid.*

104 *Bangkok Post*: "Thailand remains a nest of corruption"; 2 Jan, 2011.

105 World Food Programme.

106 Human Rights Watch: "Vietnam's Human Rights Defenders", 23 Mar, 2010.

107 *Ibid.*

108 The Heritage Foundation: 2011 Index of Economic Freedom.

109 Human Rights Watch: "Vietnam's Human Rights Defenders", 23 Mar, 2010.

110 The Heritage Foundation: 2011 Index of Economic Freedom.

Chapter 3: Africa

111 Rural Poverty Portal; "Rural Poverty in Angola"; International Fund for Agricultural Development.

112 *Ibid.*

113 CIA-The World Factbook.

114 *Ibid.*

115 International Fund for Agricultural Development: "Rural Poverty in Angola"; Rural Poverty Portal.

116 Reuters; "Rights group urges Angola to act on corruption", 13 Apr, 2010.

117 Human Rights Watch; "Transparency and Accountability in Angola"; 13 Apr, 2010.

118 *Ibid.*

119 *Ibid.*

120 *Ibid.*

121 *Ibid.*

122 *Ibid.*

123 *Ibid.*

124 *Ibid.*

125 *Ibid.*

126 UNDP in Angola: Poverty Reduction, 23 Jan, 2011.

127 *Ibid.*

128 CIA Factbook; Angola; economy.

129 Human Rights Watch; "Transparency and Accountability in Angola"; 13 Apr, 2010.

130 CIA Factbook: Angola; Economy.

131 The Heritage Foundation: 2011 Index of Economic Freedom.

132 CIA-The World Factbook.

133 The World Food Programme.

134 Human Rights Watch: 2011 World Report.

135 *Ibid.*

136 The Heritage Foundation: 2011 Index of Economic Freedom.

137 *Ibid.*

138 *Ibid.*

139 *Ibid.*

140 The Heritage Foundation: 2011 Index of Economic Freedom.

141 *Ibid.*

142 Us Dept of State: 2010 Report on Human Trafficking.

143 The Heritage Foundation: 2011 Index of Economic Freedom.

144 The Heritage Foundation: 2011 Index of Economic Freedom.

145 The World Food Programme.

146 US Dept of State: 2010 Report on Human Trafficking.

147 The Heritage Foundation: 2011 Index of Economic Freedom.

148 *Ibid.*

149 Reuters: "Congo-driven war crisis kills 45000 a month study"; 22 Jan, 2007.

150 Globalsecurity.org: "Congo Civil War".

151 Polgreen, Lydia: "Congo's Death Rate Unchanged Since War Ended"; *The New York Times*; 23 Jan, 2008.

152 Robin Wright Penn and John Prendergast. "Cell phones and Congo's war against women." The San Francisco Chronicle, 7 Jan, 2009.

153 www.iraqbodycount.org.

154 CIA-The World Factbook.

155 Smith, David; "Congo rebels raped women and babies near UN base"; *The Guardian*; 24 Aug, 2010.

156 Drc.ushahidi.com; "8 Rebels killed in attack on UN base in Rwindi, N. Kivu; 12 Jan, 2011.

157 Im-mining.com; "Mafia-style operations in DRC tin and tantalum mines"; 12 Mar, 2010.

158 Ma, Tiffany: "China and Congo's Coltan Connection"; p 3.

159 Wikipedia; Coltan.

160 Ma, Tiffany: "China and Congo's Coltan Connection"; p 4.

161 RAID; Chinese Mining Operations in Katanga, Democratic Republic of Congo, 2009 Report.

162 *Ibid*, p 9.

163 Clark, Simon; "China Lets Child Workers Die Digging in Congo Mines for Copper"; *Bloomberg.com*; 22 July, 2008.

164 *Ibid.*

165 *Ibid.*

166 In2eastafrica.net; "Kenya and DRC deal to fight illegal gold trade"; 4 Mar, 2011.

167 Odhiambo, Allan; "Dubai cartels linked to gold smuggling in Kenya"; *Business* Daily; 7 Mar, 2011.

168 Manews.com; "Minerals financing FDLR with millions of dollars"; 21 July, 2009.

169 "DR Congo Army 'works with rebels'"; *BBC News*; 10 Sep, 2008.

170 CASM: "Briefing Note: Artisanal and Small Scale Mining in The Democratic Republic of Congo"; 17 Aug, 2007, p 17.

171 "DR Congo Army 'works with rebels'"; *BBC News*; 10 Sep, 2008.

172 CASM: "Briefing Note: Artisanal and Small Scale Mining in The Democratic Republic of Congo"; 17 Aug, 2007, p 17.

173 Diamondempowerment.org; Democratic Republic of Congo / Diamond Empowerment Fund.

174 Wild, Franz: "Suicidaire Gunmen Stalk Diamond Diggers in Congo's Mining Hub"; *Bloomberg.com*; 19 May, 2009.

175 CASM: "Briefing Note: Artisanal and Small Scale Mining in The Democratic Republic of Congo"; 17 Aug, 2007, p 15.

176 *Ibid.*

177 Lubamba, Jean-Baptiste; *Modern Day Slaves*, 2007, p 5.

178 Reuters: "Angola says Congo immigrants threaten diamond sector"; 3 Aug, 2009.

179 Brilliantearth.com; "Conflict Diamond Trade in Africa and South America".

180 CASM: "Briefing Note: Artisanal and Small Scale Mining in The Democratic Republic of Congo"; 17 Aug, 2007, p 6.

181 Lubamba, Jean-Baptiste; *Modern Day Slaves*, 2007, p 7.

182 *Ibid.*

183 CASM: "Briefing Note: Artisanal and Small Scale Mining in The Democratic Republic of Congo"; 17 Aug, 2007, p 8.

184 CASM: "Briefing Note: Artisanal and Small Scale Mining in The Democratic Republic of Congo"; 17 Aug, 2007, pp 9-10.

185 The Heritage Foundation; 2011 Index of Economic Freedom.

186 *Ibid.*

187 *Ibid.*

188 Keane, Fergal; *BBC News*; "Kenya's poor at each other's throats"; 23 Jan 2008.

189 Library of Congress; Country Profile, 2007.

190 *BBC News*; "Deadly game of Kenya's gem trade"; 14 Aug, 2009.

191 Mwachiro, Kevin; "Kenya corruption costs government dearly"; *BBC News*; 3 Dec, 2010.

192   CIA-The World Factbook.

193   US Dept of State; 2010 Report on Human Trafficking.

194   Change.org; "Tell Firestone to Play Fair in Liberia!"; 16 Feb 2011.

195   *Antwerp Facets*; "Liberians losing millions of dollars annually due to illegal mining"; 27 Apr 2009.

196   US Dept of State; Background Note: Liberia.

197   Smith, David: "Military junta seizes power in Niger coup"; *The Guardian*, 19 Feb, 2010.

198   The Heritage Foundation: 2011 Index of Economic Freedom.

199   US Dept of State: 2011 International Narcotics Control Strategy Report (INCSR).

200   CIA-The World Factbook.

201   US Dept of State: 2011 International Narcotics Control Strategy Report (INCSR).

202   The Heritage Foundation: 2011 Index of Economic Freedom.

203   Human Rights Watch: World Report 2011.

204   *Ibid.*

205   Asokan, Shyamantha: "Quietly, the Christian-Muslim killing continues in Nigeria". *The Christian Science Monitor*, 25 May, 2010.

206   *Ibid.*

207   *Ibid.*

208   Human Rights Watch: World Report 2011.

209   *Ibid.*

210   *Ibid.*

211   US Dept of State: 2011 International Narcotics Control Strategy Report (INCSR).

212   The Heritage Foundation: 2011 Index of Economic Freedom.

213   CIA-The World Factbook.

214   US Dept of State: 2011 International Narcotics Control Strategy Report (INCSR).

215   CIA-The World Factbook.

216 The Heritage Foundation; 2011 Index of Economic Freedom.

217 Network Movement for Justice & Development; "Sierra Leone's Parliament ratifies illegal mining agreement that is bad for the country's development"; 24 Mar 2010.

218 The Heritage Foundation; 2011 Index of Economic Freedom.

219 CIA-The World Factbook.

220 Heritage Foundation; 2011 Index of Economic Freedom.

221 *Ibid.*

222 southafrica.info: "South Africa's new priority crimes unit"; 10 July 2009.

223 CIA-The World Factbook.

224 *Ibid.*

225 Heritage Foundation; 2011 Index of Economic Freedom.

226 CIA Factbook.

227 *The Guardian*; "Corruption endemic in Uganda"; 13 Mar, 2009.

228 Slater, Meredith; "How government corruption in Uganda is killing 300 People a Day"; *Change.org* News; 3 Oct, 2010.

229 Bavier, Joe; "Ugandan LRA rebels kill 22 in congo raids"; *Reuters:Africa*; 11, Jan 2009.

230 *UN News Centre*; "Uganda rebels murder, rape, mutilate, displace thousands in DR Congo"; 21 Dec 2009.

231 *BBC News*; "Uganda LRA rebels on massive forced recruitment drive"; 12 Aug 2010.

232 *The Guardian*; "Corruption endemic in Uganda"; 13 Mar, 2009.

233 CIA—The World Factbook.

234 *Ibid.*

235 The Heritage Foundation: 2011 Index of Economic Freedom.

236 *Ibid.*

237 US Dept of State: 2011 International Narcotics Control Strategy Report (INCSR).

238 *Ibid.*

239 upi.com; "Mugabe wants sanctions removed"; 18 Dec, 2010.

240 The Heritage Foundation: 2011 Index of Economic Freedom.

241 *Ibid.*

242 Human Rights Watch: World Report 2011.

243 US Dept of State: 2010 Report on Human Trafficking.

244 Human Rights Watch: World Report 2011.

245 *Ibid.*

246 *Ibid.*

247 *Ibid.*

248 *Ibid.*

249 The Heritage Foundation; 2011 Index of Economic Freedom.

250 Monstersandcritics.com: "EU prolongs Zimbabwe sanctions, but takes some officials of list"; 15 Feb. 2011.

251 CIA-The World Factbook.

Chapter 4: The Greater Middle East

252 Wikipedia: 2010-2011 North Africa and Middle East Protests.

253 CIA- The World Factbook.

254 The Heritage Foundation: 2011 Index of Economic Freedom.

255 *Ibid.*

256 *Ibid.*

257 *Ibid.*

258 *Ibid.*

259 *Ibid.*

260 CIA-The World Factbook.

261 *Ibid.*

262 US Dept of State; 2010 Report on Human Trafficking.

263 CIA-The World Factbook.

264 The Heritage Foundation: 2011 Index of Economic Freedom.

265 *Ibid.*

266 CIA-The World Factbook.

267 The Heritage Foundation: 2011 Index of Economic Freedom.

268 CIA-The World Factbook.

269 The Heritage Foundation: 2011 Index of Economic Freedom.

270 CIA-The World Factbook.

271 *Ibid.*

272 Chene, Marie; "Overview of Corruption in Pakistan"; U4 Expert Answer; 8 Aug, 2008.

273 *Ibid.*

274 *Ibid.*

275 *Ibid.*

276 *Ibid.*

277 The Heritage Foundation; 2011 Index of Economic Freedom.

278 US Dept of State; Trafficking in Humans Report 2010.

279 *Ibid.*

280 *Ibid.*

281 US Dept of State: 2011 International Narcotics Control Strategy Report (INCSR).

282 "UN envoy decries waste dumping off Somalia". Middle-east-online.com; 26 July, 2008.

283 Hari, Johann: "You are being lied to about pirates". *The Independent (London)*; 5 Jan, 2009.

284 Gill, Sharon: "Maritime Piracy Costs Global Community 12 Billion a Year." Eyefortransport.com; 20 Jan, 2011.

285 *Ibid.*

286 *Ibid.*

287 CIA- The World Factbook.

288 FAO: The State of Food Insecurity in the World 2008.

289 CIA- The World Factbook.

290 UN Human Development Report 2010.

291 CIA-The World Factbook.

292 Transparency International; Corruption Perceptions Index 2010.

293 Copnall, James; "Can Sudan's oil feed north and south?"; *BBC News*; 6 Jan, 2011.

294 *Sudan Tribune*; "Sudan, China agree to invest in solar energy"; 22 Dec, 2010.

295 Sayani, Daniel; "Red China increases investments and influence in Sudan"; *The New American*; 31 Jan, 2011.

296 *Afrique Avenir*; "Sudan lures Russian firms to invest in infrastructure, energy projects"; 21 Feb, 2011.

297 Allafrica.com; "Sudan Minister of Mining Talks With Russina Ambassador On Joint Cooperation in Mineral Domains"; 27 Nov, 2010.

298 The Heritage Foundation: 2011 Index of Economic Freedom.

299 *Ibid.*

300 CIA-The World Factbook.

301 *Ibid.*

302 *Ibid.*

303 *Ibid.*

304 The Heritage Foundation: 2011 Index of Economic Freedom.

305 *Ibid.*

306 *Ibid.*

307 CIA-The World Factbook.

308 *Ibid.*

309 The World Food Programme.

310 Human Rights Watch: 2011 World Report.

311 The Heritage Foundation: 2011 Index of Economic Freedom.

Chapter 5: Europe

312 The Heritage Foundation: 2011 Index of Economic Freedom.

313 CIA-The World Factbook.

314 *Ibid.*

315 *Ibid.*

316 *Ibid.*

317 *Ibid.*

318 Paddock, R.C.; "The KGB Rises Again in Russia"; *The Los Angeles Times*; 12 Jan, 2000.

319 Finn, Peter; "In Russia, a Secretive Force Widens"; *The Washington Post*; 12 Dec, 2006.

320 Albats, Evgenia; "Siloviks in power; fears or reality?"; *Echoes of Moscow*; 4 Feb, 2006.

321 US Dept of State; Report on Human Trafficking, 2010.

322 "N Koreans toiling in Russia's timber camps"; *BBC News*; 26 Aug, 2009.

323 *Ibid.*

324 *Ibid.*

325 CIA-The World Factbook.

326 *Ibid.*

327 The Heritage Foundation: 2011 Index of Economic Freedom.

328 *Ibid.*

Chapter 6: Drugs in the Americas

329 Heritage Foundation; 2011 Index of Economic Freedom.

330 US Dept of State; 2010 Report on Human Trafficking.

331 2011 International Narcotics Control Strategy Report (INCSR).

332 *Ibid.*

333 *Ibid.*

334 The Heritage Foundation: 2011 Index of Economic Freedom.

335 *Ibid.*

336 US Dept of State: 2011 International Narcotics Control Strategy Report (INCSR).

337 The Heritage Foundation: 2011 Index of Economic Freedom.

338 CIA- The World Factbook.

339 Plan Australia- Brazil.

340 US Dept of State: 2010 Report on Human Trafficking.

341 CIA- The World Factbook.

342 2011 International Narcotics Control Strategy Report (INCSR).

343 Ibid.

344 Ibid.

345 US Dept of State; 2010 Report on Human Trafficking.

346 Ibid.

347 UN News Centre; "Violent struggle over illegal mining in Colombia forces hundreds to flee"; 17 Mar 2011.

348 US Dept of State; 2010 Report on Human Trafficking.

349 The Heritage Foundation; 2011 Index of Economic Freedom.

350 2011 International Narcotics Control Strategy Report (INCSR).

351 CIA- The World Factbook.

352 World Bank.

353 US Dept of State; 2010 Report on Human Trafficking.

354 The Heritage Foundation: 2011 Index of Economic Freedom.

355 US Dept of State; 2011 International Narcotics Control Strategy Report (INCSR).

356 Ibid.

357 The Heritage Foundation; 2011 Index of Economic Freedom.

358 Dominican Today; "Over 2 million Dominicans suffer from hunger"; 7 Feb, 2007.

359 CIA-The World Factbook.

360 US Dept of State: 2011 International Narcotics Control Strategy Report (INCSR).

361 ABC News; "El Salvador's police chief resigns over corruption claims"; 24 Aug 2008.

362 Gutiérrez, Raúl; "Leftist Govt clamps down on corruption"; *IPS*; 23 Jun 2009.

363 Heritage Foundation; 2011 Index of Economic Freedom.

364 The World Food Programme.

365 CIA- The World Factbook.

366 US Dept of State; 2010 Report on Human Trafficking.

367 US Dept of State: 2011 International Narcotics Control Strategy Report (INCSR).

368 *Ibid.*

369 *Ibid.*

370 *Ibid.*

371 *Ibid.*

372 *Ibid.*

373 *Ibid.*

374 *Ibid.*

375 Gould, Jens Erik; "Haiti Earthquake Damage to Cost $7.8 Billion, Un's Barcena Says"; *Bloomberg*; 20 Mar, 2010.

376 CIA—The World Factbook.

377 The Heritage Foundation; 2011 Index of Economic Freedom.

378 World Bank.

379 Eurasianminerals.com/new/Haiti.

380 CIA—The World Factbook.

381 2011 International Narcotics Control Strategy Report (INCSR).

382 The Heritage Foundation; 2011 Index of Economic Freedom.

383 CIA—The World Factbook.

384 *Ibid.*

385 Morgan, Scott, "Jamaica says it can win its drug war for $1billion"; stopthedrugwar.org; 3 June, 2010.

386 US Dept of State: 2011 International Narcotics Control Strategy Report (INCSR).

387 CIA- The World Factbook.

388 The Heritage Foundation; 2011 Index of Economic Freedom.

389 US Dept of State: 2011 International Narcotics Control Strategy Report (INCSR).

390 Siddique, Haroon: "Mexico drug wars have killed 35,000 people in four years". *The Guardian UK*; 13 Jan 2011.

391 Ioan Grillo & San Francisco del Rincon: "Mexico's Ex-Leader Vicente Fox: Legalize Drugs to End War". *Time*; 19 Jan 2011.

392 *Ibid.*

393 US Dept of State: 2011 International Narcotics Control Strategy Report (INCSR).

394 *Ibid.*

395 *Ibid.*

396 Coronel, Gustav; "The Corruption of Democracy in Venezuela"; *USA Today*, Mar 2008.

397 *Ibid.*

398 *Ibid.*

399 *Ibid.*

400 *Ibid.*

401 chinamining.org; "Venezuela inks new oil deal with Chinese firms", 22 Mar 2011.

402 *Ibid.*

403 Gupta, Girish; "Venezuela's State Oil Company Under the Spotlight Yet Again"; Minyanville.com, 23 Mar 2011.

404 *Ibid.*

405 McElroy, Damien; "Chavez pushes Venezuela into food war"; *The Telegraph*, 23 Jun 2010.

406 *The Economist;* "Venezuela Socialism: Food Fight", 10 Jun 2010.

407 Gupta, Girish; "Venezuela's State Oil Company Under the Spotlight Yet Again"; Minyanville.com, 23 Mar 2011.

408 *Ibid.*

409 Devereaux, Charlie; "Chavez's Seizures Scuttle Housing Campaign as Venezuelan Steel Output Sags"; *Bloomberg*; 17 Dec 2010.

410 Minaya, Ezequiel; "Venezuela's Housing Minister Reports Shortage Not Yet Addressed"; *Wall Street Journal*, 17 Feb 2011.

411 *Ibid.*

412 Devereaux, Charlie; "Chavez's Seizures Scuttle Housing Campaign as Venezuelan Steel Output Sags"; *Bloomberg*; 17 Dec 2010.

413 Reuters; "Venezuela blackouts from bad planning, drought", 18 Jan 2010.

414 US Dept of State; 2010 Report on Human Trafficking.

415 *NYTimes*; "Chávez foe accuses him of allowing leftist Colombian Rebels"; 11 Nov 2009.

416 2011 International Narcotics Control Strategy Report (INCSR).

417 *Ibid.*

418 *Ibid.*

419 Hawley, Chris; "Venezuela drug trade booms"; *USA Today*; 21 July 2010.

420 2011 International Narcotics Control Strategy Report (INCSR).

421 CIA- The World Factbook.

Afterword

What this book ultimately proves is that money is here to stay, and it's important to keep after the confidence tricksters. Clearly, fraudulent money transactions will not improve living conditions for anyone except criminals. That being said, there's some pretty solid political and economic advice in this book. Don't forget—free booze and free digital downloads just might be the best part of this socioeconomic theory!